The Prehistoric Sites of Montgomeryshire

Monuments in the Landscape

Volume XI

The Prehistoric Sites of Montgomeryshire

by
Beth McCormack

Logaston Press

LOGASTON PRESS
Little Logaston Woonton Almeley
Herefordshire HR3 6QH
logastonpress.co.uk

First published by Logaston Press 2006
Copyright © Beth McCormack 2006

ISBN 1 904396 32 1

Set in Times by Logaston Press
and printed in Great Britain by
The Cromwell Press, Trowbrdige, Wilts.

*Dedicated to Russell Chaffee
and all warm, loving fauna.*

For me there were no paths at all. Thickets, ditches, ponds, labyrinths, morasses, but no paths. (M. Atwood, *Lady Oracle*).

Please Note

Many of the monuments mentioned in this book are situated on private land and permission from the owner must, therefore, be obtained before visiting them.

The following points should also be observed:

1. When visiting sites in the countryside, always follow the Countryside Code.
2. On all sites, extreme care should be taken.
3. Any artefacts found on sites should be reported to the nearest museum or the Clwyd-Powys Archaeological Trust, 7a Church Street, Welshpool, Powys, SY21 7DL. Tel: 01938 553670.
4. Under no circumstances should visitors dig on or around any site. Any damage could result in prosecution.
5. It is an offence under the 1979 Ancient Monuments and Archaeological Areas Act to use metal detectors on or near scheduled ancient monuments. In addition, simple 'treasure hunting' near ancient monuments can damage evidence to such an extent that archaeologists are unable to interpret it fully in the future.

Acknowledgments

Thanks to everyone who supported and encouraged this book: Mom, Dad, Suzanne and Kara McCormack of the McCormack clan; Jeff, Ian, Ms. Jenny, Bill, Chris and Rich at CPAT; Priscilla Inkpen, Steven Taylor, Reed Bye, Alan Hartway, Jason, Liz, Lily, Holly, Jeff, Jamba, Antonia and Suzi at Naropa University; John Allemand, Marisol, Jane, Guideaux, Dave and Megan in New Orleans; Ms. Elaine and everyone at the Pinewood Tavern; Julian Thomas and Richard Bradley for never-ending inspiration; Andy Johnson and Andrew Selkirk for their confidence; Dr. John McNabb and my favourite warm, loving fauna: Chicken, Birdie, Nina and Wiggles.

For permission to use the illustrations on pages 34, 41, 42, 43, 63, 67, 70, 84, 94, 98, 149 and 150, grateful thanks are given to Frances Lynch, the drawings being taken from her book *Prehistoric Wales*. In addition thanks are given to the National Museum of Wales for the originals of food vessels 1 and 3 on page 67, and the items on pages 84 and 98, and likewise Colin Burgess for those on page 70, all of which were redrawn by Frances Lynch; Alex Gibson for the pottery on pages 41 and 42 which were in turn were used by Frances Lynch from his publications; and likewise Bill Britnell for the plan on page 94 used from the excavation report. For permission to use the photographs on pages 53, 55, 103, 104, 109, 128, 131, 134, 135, 138, 144, 145, and 147 grateful thanks are given to CPAT (and also for their help in providing distribution maps), and to the National Museum of Wales for that on page 90. The photographs on pages 35, 47, 60, 61, 77, 102, 106, 113, 115, 118, 120, 126 and 154 are the author's; those on pages 76, 116, 117, 119, 122, 123, 125, 127, 136, 139 and 141 belong to Logaston Press.

Beth McCormack   March 2006

Other titles in the Monuments in the Landscape series

Contents

The Stone Age

Introduction

Homo rudolfensis and *Homo habilis* (dated to at least 2.5 million years ago in Africa) were the first bipedal hominids—scavengers and foragers who also developed stone tool technology. These tools were probably used not for hunting or butchering, but to process tough, woody plant foods for easier digestion. Early *Homo* developed into *Homo ergaster* around 2 million years ago. *Homo erectus* spilt off from *Ergaster* and by 1.8 million years ago had travelled across Europe into Asia whilst *Ergaster* remained in Africa. *Homo erectus* colonized much of the subtropical Old World with only a rudimentary tool technology and without the benefit of language, symbolic culture or individual consciousness as we know it.

By 1.6 to 1.4 million years ago African tool technology had developed into the Acheulian industry which was carried to Europe by *Homo heidelbergensis*, another descendant of *Homo ergaster*, about 600,000 years ago. *Homo heidelbergensis* is thought to be the common ancestor of *Homo sapiens* in Africa and *Homo neanderthalensis* in Europe between 250,000 and 200,000 years ago. *Homo sapiens* appears to have had an early advanced technology, resembling the much later Upper Palaeolithic of Europe. *Homo sapiens* migrated throughout the world, eventually becoming the sole survivor of all the hominid species.

In order to understand how human activity developed in Britain it is important to realize the impact of glaciation on the landscape. The Pleistocene Epoch comprises a series of advancing and retreating ice caps. Of the four recognized periods of glaciation only three—the Anglian, Wolstonian and Devensian Glacials—

Date range BC	Glacial Stage	Human activity	Archaeological industries & (sites)
500–400,000	Anglian	Lower Paleolithic: First occupation of Britain	Cromerian (Boxgrove)
400–370,000	Hoxnian Interglacial		Acheulean Clactonian (Swanscombe)
370–120,000	Wolstonian		Levallois (Pontnewydd)
150–60,000		Human absence	
120-80,000	Ipswichian Intergalcial		
80–10,000	Devensian	Middle to Upper Palaeolithic transition Human absence between then recolonisation after the Late Glacial maximum	Mousterian Aurignacian Gravettian Creswellian (Ffynnon Beuno, Paviland, Pin Hole, Creswell Crags)
10–4,000	Holocene (or Flandrian)	Final Upper Palaeolithic Mesolithic	(Gough's Cave)

Table showing relationship between glacial stages and human activity have left physical traces in Britain. These glacials were punctuated by warm periods known as Interglacials, and even during these, sporadic climate changes occurred periodically. (A temperate spell within a glacial period is known as an interstadial, while a cold spell within an interglacial period is known as a stadial.)

During the maximum cold portions of each glacial phase, occupation of Britain would have been impossible while the temperate climate during interstadials easily supported human habitation. Additionally, long transitional phases existed between the glacial and interglacial maxima where less extreme conditions allowed occupation in Britain. During these transitional phases, as during full glacial conditions, much of the earth's water froze into glaciers, resulting in lower sea levels. Britain would then have been at the west end of a vast plain connecting the country with the northern European coastline and with Scandinavia to the east. At these times the landscape of Britain was open steppe, arctic tundra or covered in sheets of ice. During warmer periods, sea level rose, Britain became an island, reforestation occurred and animals more suited to those conditions began to spread north.

The earliest period of human existence in Britain is known as the Lower Palaeolithic and runs from 500,000 BC until 50,000 BC (in Wales 225,000 BC to 50,000 BC), a period that includes the Anglian and Wolstonian Glacials, as well as the start of the Devensian Glacial. Occupation was intermittent based on access and climate conditions, with long periods of no habitation at all. Settlement was mainly restricted to open landscapes that included river valleys and other waterside sites. Groups of people were highly mobile within their selected regions, settling in short-term, favourable locations rather than permanent home bases. Survival depended on a technology of stone and flint tools, fire and a subsistence strategy consisting of scavenging, hunting smaller and possibly larger prey and foraging wild plant foods. Stone tools were made with local materials. Fire was managed by this time, though there is no evidence of well-built fireplaces or hearths at campsites.

The earliest known human sites in Britain date to the period just before the Anglian Glacial and are located across southern England. Occupation of sites was temporary and opportunistic—when conditions were favourable and routes accessible. All the sites were close to water and local caves were probably not occupied. At the height of the following Anglian glaciation, occupation of Britain would have been impossible, as there were ice fronts all the way down to the area now occupied by London. These ice sheets obliterated the former Cromerian landscape, doubtlessly including evidence of human activity.

Occupation of Britain then expanded during the following Hoxnian interglacial period around 370,000 years ago. Deciduous woodland recovered in Britain along with open grassland. Large herds of herbivores roamed the landscape along with carnivores that included wolves and leopards. Over 3,000 findspots of Hoxnian Interglacial and early successive Wolstonian Glacial dates in Britain suggest a high population or frequent visitation (Darvill). Occupation is once again centred on eastern and southern parts of Britain. Preferred occupation sites included river valleys, lake margins, and both forested and open landscapes, even some upland areas. Some locales were revisited repeatedly. This period is dominated by two industrial tool traditions: the fairly crude Clactonian, non-biface tradition; and the Acheulian bi-face tradition. Clactonian tools were flakes of flint struck off a core which was eventually discarded or worked to a rough edge for use as a chopper. Acheulian tools were made by flaking a core of flint (or other fine-grained rock) into the desired form, called a bi-face due to it having two worked faces. With this technology it was the flakes rather than the cores that were discarded, or trimmed for use as cutters (Darvill). The tool kit comprised the hand-axe, hammer, scraper, cleaver and cutter used in butchery, woodworking and plant processing. There is also evidence for the use of fire, possibly to clear land. Humans continued to be highly mobile, probably following the herds on their seasonal migrations. Britain may have been abandoned at the height of this interglacial as forest cover would have been too dense, restricting the movement of the herds and confining human movement to dangerous game trails. However there is some evidence at Beeches Pit and Barnham in Suffolk for human presence during this fully temperate environment attesting to the settlers' versatility.

There is little evidence of human activity during the height of the Wolstonian Glacial when Britain was again locked in major ice sheets, although some has been recorded in the east of England during the more moderate interstadial climates.

The sudden appearance of Levallois technology around 300,000 years ago as the climate was cooling toward the full glacial maximum in Britain represents an important cultural change. The Levallois technique was to prepare a block of flint by surface flaking one face to reach a point where flakes of predetermined size and shape could be struck from the prepared block, a complex technique. The technique was used to produce a variety of tools, including hand-axes probably used for butchery, sharp flakes perhaps used for cutting meat, blades and triangular points possibly used to tip spears, and stone scrapers for use in preparation of hides. The technology first appears at Baker's Hole (Northfleet, Kent), thought to be the birthplace of the industry, but did not replace the preceding Acheulean industry, instead appearing in association with it. This sophisticated and efficient new tool kit probably reflects wider social change, including, some believe, linguistic capabilities.

Fascinating insights into this Lower Palaeolithic society are provided by evidence recovered from the Pontnewydd limestone cave overlooking the rich Vale of Clwyd in Wales. Bone evidence shows that herds of bison and horse roamed the steppes, whilst the transitional climate between temperate and glacial also supported bear, rhinoceros, wolf, and leopard. Twenty human bone fragments were found, mostly jaw shards and teeth, representing at least four individuals and possibly as many as seven, of whom five were juveniles (Aldhouse-Green 1995) belonging to an early species of *Homo neanderthalensis*. No structures, hearths or living floors were found here, or anywhere else in Wales for that matter, and the remains may indicate a single accumulation or disposal of a group or groups over time. Deposition may have been formal or by chance, simultaneous or successive, or even an accumulation of carnivore kills. Tools recovered were of the Levallois type, made of materials from distant sources suggesting either long distance travel by the group or trade. Alternatively the material may have been brought from afar by glacial or peri-glacial action, and the tools made on the spot. There is evidence of deliberate selection of raw materials by the Pontnewydd hominids for use as tools based on size and flaking characteristics of the rocks (Lynch *et al*). There is no evidence of re-sharpening, indicating short term use. However, the elegance and precision of the tools indicate that these particular stone knappers were experienced and had considerable skill in the latest technology.

Overall, archaeologists believe that the Pontnewydd cave was used as a transitory or seasonal campsite, probably as part of a hunting strategy in which local raw materials were used for the production of temporary, improvised tool-kits. The fact that this evidence survived the scouring activities of later glacial ice-sheets is remarkable.

During this period the population in Wales was very low, probably only numbering 1-2,000 people (Gamble *et al.* 1999). They would have operated in dispersed and highly mobile groups, probably based on familial ties. Stray finds attest temporary settlement, with no evidence for permanent houses. Society was likely egalitarian, there being no evidence of hierarchy or wealth accumulation—artefacts deposited with burials appear to be of roughly equal value.

Alongside early technological evidence, there is some evidence for the very early origin of symbolic behaviour, art and religion in the Lower Palaeolithic, mostly through the use of ochre. Ochre is powdered haematite and is dark red, considered by some cultures to be the 'blood of the earth' (Rudgeley). It has been found in many ceremonial contexts, particularly burials, and is still in use today both ritually and therapeutically. As for art, the oldest known figurine to be accepted by the archaeological community is the Berekhat Ram, a small yellowish brown pebble naturally shaped in a female form and embellished by artificially added grooves found at the foot of Mount Hermon in northern Israel. The oldest possible date for the figurine is 800,000 BC, though this is disputed. Though examples of artwork are rare, the evidence for creative thought is compelling.

The final phase of the Wolstonian glaciation was one of the most severe of the entire Middle Pleistocene, and there appears to have been a long period in Britain with no human contact between approximately 150,000 BC and 60,000 BC. 'Britain' was then huge, sea level being so low, creating a considerable expanse of dry land in the North Sea, with ice sheets running down to the midlands. To the south was polar desert with permafrost beyond.

Faunal and some human evidence has been collected from several sites utilised towards the end of this glaciation and the beginning of the following Ipswichian Interglacial. Gradually the landscape became covered by a large-leaved deciduous forest, and the July temperatures reached an average of about 4°C higher than the current norm. Re-occupation by Neanderthals directly followed.

Middle Palaeolithic

The final glacial period in the Pleistocene Epoch is the Devensian, the most temperate of all the epoch's glacial periods, The Middle Palaeolithic occurs during this period, dating from around 50,000 to 26,000 BC. During this period the climate was characterized by cool, arid conditions but with at least 15 warmer interstadials. Due to low sea levels, Britain was connected to Northern Europe and to eastern Russia in an unbroken expanse of dry open grassland known as Mammoth Steppe. At that time the landscape comprised both moss and shrub tundra and meadow tundra, with light snow cover melting early in the year, and a fairly long, though cool, growing season. Vegetation included nutritious herbs and grasses, dwarf shrubs, dwarf birch, dwarf willows and Juniper shrub, with very few trees. This environment was very productive, sustaining herds of large mammals. Animals included mammoth, woolly rhinoceros, horse, spotted hyena (Currant and Jacobi 1997), bison, possibly ibex, and the all-important reindeer. Ice may have been confined to Scotland or come further south to the Isle of Man. Winter temperatures were –20°C.

As few as 81 European sites are documented for this period and the evidence from Britain is sparse and clustered in a few geographic areas. This is probably a genuine reflection of settlement, with perhaps fewer than five groups of not less than 25 people (the minimum number of persons needed to sustain a reproductively viable population) in the country at any one time.

The most important event of this era is the disappearance of Neanderthal society and the appearance of anatomically modern humans. Classic Neanderthals lived until approximately 30,000 BC (and perhaps later) overlapping by approximately 70,000 years with *Homo sapiens* in Europe, many times in very close proximity to one another. Given the similarities between the species, the notion that they did not interbreed is surprising, and it is a matter of hot dispute as to whether Neanderthals were incorporated into the modern human species by interbreeding. As archaeologist Clive Gamble says of James Cook's voyages in the Pacific in the eighteenth century, quoting Shreeve: 'Cook's men would come to some distant land, and lining the shore are all these very bizarre-looking human beings with spears, long jaws, browridges. God, how odd it must have seemed to them. But that didn't stop the Cook crew from making a lot of little Cooklets. One thing you can count on with humans — whether they can interbreed or not, the first thing they do when they meet is try to find out' (Shreeve). (Interpretation of DNA analysis appears to be ambiguous, only definitely proving that no Neanderthal biology is contained within currently living humans, not that interbreeding didn't take place. Dr. Alan Templeton, an evolutionary geneticist at Washington University, has said that some hybridization may have occurred without the effects showing up in mitochondrial DNA.)

This bleak period is known as Mousterian, after the Le Moustier caves in France occupied by Neanderthals. Evidence for Mousterian activity in Wales during this period includes the intriguing Neanderthal site of Coygan Cave, a hyena den site formerly used by Neanderthals. Three Mousterian bout coupé biface hand-axes were found, made of deliberately selected local raw materials (Lynch *et al*). (The bout coupé style differs from earlier hand-axes in their u-shaped form (Darvill)). This British bout coupé may be either a local variant or the home base of the style common to what is now northern France. Older excavation records describe a possible hearth inside the cave, which would prove occupation. A Mousterian period hand-axe was also found at Lavernock, near Cardiff. All of the cave assemblages are very small, leading archaeologists to postulate periodic revisits to temporary locations on a seasonal basis by hunter-gatherer groups who occasionally lost or abandoned artefacts. Bigger caves, although not necessarily long-term occupation sites, probably represented major places in the Neanderthal mental maps of their world (McNabb).

The versatility of Mousterian Neanderthals is evidenced by their eclectic tool-making capabilities. Some cave sites, but especially open-air sites have been found to contain tools from varying and contemporaneous industries of this period including Levallois and bout coupé, laminar cores and flakes normally associated with the early Upper Palaeolithic, and even leaf-points. This may indicate earlier inception of this technology than was previously thought (see below). Neanderthals were perhaps working at the cutting edge.

The Aurignacian industry directly follows the Mousterian and is dated from approximately 40,000 to 29,000 BC. During this time flintworking technologies advanced greatly, the range of items in tool-kits increasing. Hand-axes, which had been used for the previous 200,000 years were replaced by a range of blade based (rather than flake based), task-specific tools. The most important new tool was the leaf-point, a large (10-15 cm) blade, probably used as a spear tip. Knives, scrapers and other points were also common. As can be appreciated from the finds in the cave sites mentioned above, there is some dispute as to whether this technology is one of the last expressions of Neanderthal culture in Britain or the first expressions of modern human culture. Frances Lynch suspects that this technological explosion may have arisen from 'a cultural shift fired by the interaction of two intelligent human species' — *Homo neanderthalensis* and *Homo sapiens*. Only four sites from this period have been found in Britain — three of them in Wales. Ffynnon Beuno in northern Wales is particularly interesting because of its location north of the southern Devensian ice margin, indicating that hunting parties must have reacted to glacial advance and retreat. The other two sites are at Hoyle's Mouth, Pembrokeshire, and Paviland, on the Gower peninsula.

The Gravettian period followed (roughly covering the period 30,000 to 20,000 BC) for which again evidence is slight in Britain, with only eight sites, and relies on the presence of the Font-Robert point, which has a distinctive tanged tip that resembles a dart. A single-tanged broken blade at Paviland may be Font-Robert, assigning the cave to the Gravettian. Further evidence for this assignment is the recently re-dated, fabulously celebrated Red Lady of Paviland, a *Homo sapiens* skeleton, now placed at 27,900 BC (Aldhouse-Green 2000). The Red Lady in fact turned out to be an adult male who had been placed in a shallow grave within the cave and sprinkled with red ochre. The use of ochre in burials increases

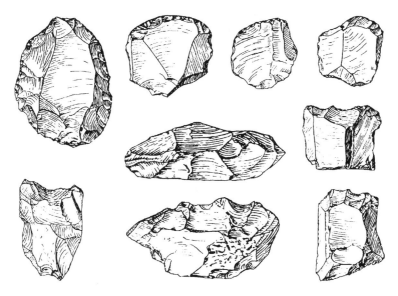

Eaxmples of flint scrapers found in Paviland Cave, Gower

at this time, though burial practice itself was still quite rare—there are just 27 known European burials with colourant in the grave. This deliberately-placed body was accompanied by a mammoth skull, two mammoth ivory rods, two ivory bracelets and a few perforated shells. Presumably, this type of funereal treatment indicates that the deceased held an important place in society, perhaps that of a shaman or tribal leader. DNA analysis of the skeleton revealed the stunning conclusion that his people, rather than migrant Neolithic farmers from the East, are the ancestors of modern Britons (Aldhouse-Green 2000).

Paviland cave was probably considered a sacred place and likely visited for ceremonial occasions. Ritual may have included shamanistic ceremony and bear-worship. Spatulae found on the site can be interpreted to resemble elements of the female body and may have significance similar to those of East European figurines (Aldhouse-Green 2000). Lynch agrees that 'the unusual and special nature of the evidence—the ceremonial burial, the unique spatulae, the ivory objects, and the continuation of visits to the site during a period of extreme climatic downturn (at a period when virtually no other evidence is known of human presence in Britain)—suggests that the cave, or perhaps the hill containing it, may have been of ancestral or religious significance and so perhaps an object of pilgrimage'.

The final occupation of the cave occurred when the Devensian was moving toward full glacial conditions. The abandonment of Britain was probably complete by the end of the Gravettian period (McNabb).

Yet this era in human history saw the emergence of individuals as creative agents (Gambel). Human innovation developed, and the period saw increasing creativity in personal ornamentation, figurines, paintings, engravings and music. Indeed, music and art burgeoned over the world. A notched mammoth bone, possibly a rasp, was discovered in Belgium dated to 50-40,000 BC. At a Middle Palaeolithic Crimean site 111 pierced animal bones, probably whistles, were discovered. Other sites have yielded bone flutes. The Austrian Galgenburg Venus, dated to 29,000 BC, is beautifully made by a technically advanced, skilled artisan. In addition, thousands of human and animal figurines were being produced at this time, whilst burials and grave goods became more common.

The Upper Palaeolithic
The Devensian Full Glacial phase dates to about 25-16,000 years ago with the most intense cold, the Late Glacial Maximum, beginning at around 20,000 BC. Britain was part of a huge basin extending across the North Sea into what is now Denmark, the Netherlands, Belgium and Northern France, and across the English Channel into western France. By 16,000 BC the ice cap covered England and Wales (Darvill). All of Europe north of the Mediterranean appears to have been abandoned by humans during the Late Glacial Maximum, with the exception of one site in southwestern France, one in north-eastern Spain and at Little Hoyle Cave, Tenby dating to 15,500 BC which has yielded an ungulate bone and flint artefacts. These may be residual from an older occupation, however.

At around 11,000 BC the Windermere or Late glacial Interstadial began, during which Britain and northern Europe became a mosaic of tundra and steppe. Steppe vegetation included dwarf versions of juniper and willow, grasses and herbs. Tundra vegetation included birch, pine and willow (Gambel). After 10,000 BC, smaller animals moved north to join the larger mammals in their periglacial environment (Darvill). The mammoth, the icon of the prehistoric landscape, became extinct around this time. Faunal evidence during the Later Devensian includes wolf, red fox, arctic fox, bear, wild cattle, elk, horse and red deer. Cold-adapted reindeer reappeared during the Loch Lomond Stadial. According to Lynch, red deer may have followed a migratory pattern of summer/upland, winter/lowland movements, however there is no evidence of summer exploitation by Palaeolithic hunters in Wales. The spring and autumn migrations of red deer were probably important because of the immensity of the herds.

Repopulation took place after 11,300 BC. This probably marks the beginning of a long period of occupation and continuing social development. Late Devensian people appear to have revisited the same locations their predecessors used prior to the glaciation including caves in the south-west, Mendips, Wales and the southern Pennines. Settlement expanded into the uplands and there were almost certainly settlements in the basin which was once southern Britain, but which are now undersea. Artefacts are sometimes brought up by fishermen.

By 9000 BC tree cover was re-establishing itself, dominated by pine and birch (Darvill). The final phase of the Late Glacial was the Loch Lomond Stadial dating between 8800 and 8000 BC. during which Britain was again covered in ice or periglacial tundra. Britain appears to have been abandoned once again, especially during the time of most intense cold between 8500 BC and 8300 BC. Re-occupation began shortly thereafter.

The British Upper Palaeolithic can be subdivided into two general periods, the first being the Late Upper Palaeolithic, characterized by the Creswellian industry (10,900-10,000 BC), named after its place of most intensive evidence in the Creswell Crags area of Derbyshire. This technology meant that leaf points were replaced by shouldered and tanged blades and gave rise to steeply retouched awls, burins and end scrapers. (A tanged blade is one that comes to a point and may be augmented by outward curving shoulders or inward curving notches on one or both sides of the blade.) Bone and antler were used more frequently. Barbed points, probably used as harpoons were an important innovation and bone was also used for awls and needles (Darvill). Archaeologist and specialist in prehistoric cognition, Stevn Mithen, postulates that the sudden use of animal products for tools reflects an important step in human cognitive evolution. Creswellian sites include Gough's Cave, Cheddar and Hoyle's Mouth, Pembrokeshire. Creswellian groups were highly mobile and most likely engaged in long distance trade in high quality flint, Baltic amber, and north European sea-shells.

Creswellian peoples occupied caves as well as open-air sites during the Late Glacial (McNabb), and the Creswell crags have yielded many artefacts as well as recently discovered cave art. Their tools are characterized by high quality trapezoidal and angled points used for blades, burins and piercers, often made from material that had been transported from distant sources, indicating the importance of quality to these stone knappers. Robin Hood's Cave was used by Creswellian hunters as an arctic hare processing and trapping site; arctic hares yielded meat, valuable pelts, sinew and tendon for string and bones suitable for awls and needles. The Church Hole cave has yielded bone needles and an awl, and perhaps most important of all, the first cave artwork known in Britain. This consists of ten clear images engraved onto the walls along with several ambiguous engraved lines. During the 20,000 year span of cave art, signs, ideomorphs, ideograms or symbols such as lines and zigzags, have always accompanied pictures of animals. Many interpret these symbols as entoptic imagery, or imagery seen during trance or hallucination. Entoptic images are common to all humans regardless of culture and one may see the same symbols depicted in the art of Europe, Africa, South America, Australia, Siberia and elsewhere (Clottes & Lewis-Williams, 1996). At the cave mouth is a 50 cm long engraving of an ibex. Seventeen metres into the cave is an engraving of four or five long-necked birds, possibly swans or geese, all facing in the same direction and upwards. This imagery may not be surprising, given the presence of swan-bone points at Creswell. There are charcoal remnants near this engraving, which could be the vestiges of a hearth providing light for the artists. Another smaller ibex and a bovid (probably bison), as well as two triangular 'vulvae' are also found in Church Hole. This art and the accompanying tool industry were clearly influenced by continental practice, for there is no evidence of ibex presence in this area of Britain in the Late Pleistocene. Whilst the depiction of the ibex could reflect a folk memory or a fortunate glimpse across the plains of a rare and faintly familiar beast, it more likely indicates highly mobile peoples who covered vast geographical distances if not annually then at least in the course of their life.

Another cave at Creswell Crags known as Pin Hole yielded a bone engraved with a humanoid figure with an animal's head (Pettitt). This half-human/half-beast has many parallels all over the world, and is usually attributed to shamanistic ceremony. It probably reflects the practices of the people then making use of the area that is now Montgomeryshire. Shamanism is defined as the religious expression of a nomadic era of hunter-gatherers (Drury), and is common to cultures all over the globe. The shaman enters a trance state during which time he may traverse the cosmos and speak to ancestors and spirits on behalf of the community. Animals play a pivotal role in Shamanism and are depicted in almost all shamanic art. The art at Church Hole is important to the understanding of past as well as future religious practice in Britain. Parietal Art scholars interpret the rock face as a veil between this world and spirit world. The engraving or paint created a link between person, rock and spirit world (Clottes & Lewis-Williams, 1996). Caves are thought to symbolize the mother, creation, death and rebirth. Caves were also passageways to the lowest tier of the three-tiered shamanic cosmos, which includes the underworld, this world, and the heavens. Inside a cave, people were completely surrounded by the underworld and everything that took place there became highly charged.

Ceremonies led by a shaman or other clan elite were likely conducted in these decorated caves. If the ceremony were held at the cave mouth, many members of the community would be able to attend, so it makes sense that areas near the entrance or other large chambers within the caves would be embellished, and this is indeed the case. These communal chambers were like modern churches reinforcing the status of the shaman/artists. Being inside a cave, these displays of religious and economic power were mysterious yet conspicuous. The artwork enabled the shaman to enforce conformity of religious belief among the community. This is important as originality and individuality challenge religious and political status quo (Clottes & Lewis-Williams, 1996).

The location of the long-necked bird engravings in a small, dark chamber at Church Hole is significant. Most decorated caves contain depictions located in small, dark openings at a distance from the entrance and accessed by winding tunnels. Some paintings/engravings are located in tiny recesses or high on the rock face and accessed only by climbing. It is clear that these depictions are meant to be viewed by one or two people at a time. These may have been vision-quest locations for initiates. These dark, isolated chambers can cause sensory deprivation if inhabited for long periods of time, which is one way of entering a trance state.

Passages among decorated caves may contain scattered and grouped images marking transitional thresholds. Some, like Church Hole have no images at all. Even these undecorated passages appear symbolic, possibly representing the birth canal. Passages remain significant as religion develops in Britain; for example the design of Neolithic passage graves directly echoes these decorated caves. They both include a large communal area, a passage, and a small, dark chamber for those privileged to enter the inner sanctum and learn its mysteries. Perhaps not surprisingly, passage graves are the only tombs found containing art, particularly spirals. Both the cave and the tomb represent descent into the underworld, death and rebirth. The portal is the border between the world of the dead and the world of the living.

During this Creswellian period, long distance trade developed dramatically across Britain. Transportation of goods over quite long distances have been recorded, including flint from Holy Cross Mountains, Poland (400 km) and fossil amber from the Black Sea (700 km) (Lynch *et al*). No house sites have been found in Wales for this phase of human development, and groups continued to be small and highly mobile, and based on familial ties.

The second phase of the British Upper Palaeolithic is known as the Final Upper Palaeolithic (10,000-8000 BC), comprising several lithic industries. The most prevalent advancements were the introduction of pen-knife points for archery, long blades of 12 cm in length or more, along with continued use of the Creswellian tool industry. The spread of the bow as a technology is associated from 10,000 BC onwards with more forested environments in north-western Europe (McNabb), whilst 28 'long blade' sites have been found in Britain, mostly in the south and east and in river valleys or low-lying lands close to flint sources.

Activity along the Welsh Marches is evidenced by stray finds including a barbed antler spearpoint from Porth-y-Waen, Shropshire dated to 9,390 +/- 120 BC. During the Final Upper Palaeolithic, communities were more localized and smaller scale. For the most part Wales was abandoned once again during the intensely cold Younger Dryas phase, with the only evidence for human presence appearing at Kendrick's Cave and Parc Cwm, Gower. Open sites during this time include Llanishen, Gwernvale, New Radnor and Breidden. These may have been temporary hunting camps, as they are strategically located along migration routes.

Evidence of advanced mathematical/symbolic thinking comes from the Late Devensian site of Gough's Cave in Cheddar Gorge which has yielded the richest collection of organic artefacts bearing deliberate incisions yet found in Britain. A large rib segment bears a number of engraved criss-crossing lines on one face and groups of incisions along the edges of another. According to Alexander Marshack, these lines may reflect an artificial memory system ('notation' or 'tallying'). This may be a calendar of some sort or perhaps an accounting system. The incisions found on a hare bone from the same site could indicate a quinary numerical system. Perhaps this item was a score-card or a type of calculator. If correct, this indicates an advanced grasp of numbers and the language associated therewith (Rudgeley).

In Wales, this same incised decoration has been found on three ochred roe deer metapodia (foot bones) and on several red deer, bovid and elk teeth and a horse maxilla from Kendrick's Cave, north Wales, dating to around 8000 BC. These may be grave goods associated with four human skeletons found nearby. The art bears similarities to later Palaeolithic and Mesolithic contexts reflecting a cultural continuity spanning the transition between the Pleistocene and the following Holocene epoch (Pettitt).

What appears to be an artistic renaissance was occurring throughout the world at this time. Both cave and portable art were becoming more and more common. There was also an explosion of technology including ceramics, weaving and the making of calendars. Human and animal figurines continued to be made in all parts of the globe. Phalli and vulva became popular depictions in all types of art, as well as pregnant and menstruating women, images that are procreative and regenerative rather than sexual. People of the Upper Palaeolithic were clearly developing a spirituality, after all they were a people dependent on the natural world for their survival. Some level of manipulation of events such as weather and herd movements was desirable and shamanism addressed these concerns and needs, intervening on behalf of the community with spirits and ancestors who controlled these events.

Mesolithic

The Mesolithic period in Britain dates from 10,000 BC through 4500 BC. This was a period of dramatic climate change marking the end of the Pleistocene and ringing in the Holocene recovery. This entire warming transition took only 75 years! (McNabb) Open late glacial landscapes were replaced by forests of birch and pine, ultimately giving way to oak, elm, alder and lime. Uplands were forested while higher peaks remained open. Coastal and river valley areas were open and rich in resources including grasses for grazing, raw materials for stone tools, plant-foods, reeds for basketry and thatching, and peat for fuel (Lynch *et al*), making them highly desirable occupation sites. All across Britain the horse, arctic hare and reindeer of the open late-glacial landscapes were gradually replaced by red deer, roe deer, wild cattle, aurochs (wild cattle), boar and elk. Elk subsequently disappeared, probably due to overhunting. In Wales, wild cattle and deer grazed in coastal fens and saltmarshes. Welsh sites also yield a wide variety of faunal evidence including red and roe deer, wild pig, aurochs, brown bear, wild cat or marten, fox, cervid, dog, wolf, beaver, wood mouse, bank vole, otter, birds such as coot, mallard and possible wading birds, and marine resources including eel, goby, smelt, three spined stickleback, flatfish and seals (Lynch). Plant foods including hazelnuts were consistently important in Welsh and British Mesolithic society.

From 7000–5000 BC, some 80% of Wales was forested, leaving only open river valleys and coastal areas as a habitat for herbivores. Wales seems to have been unoccupied until 7,200 BC, 500 years later than England. During the later Mesolithic the population in Wales was probably between 400 and 1,800 with the higher densities in coastal locations.

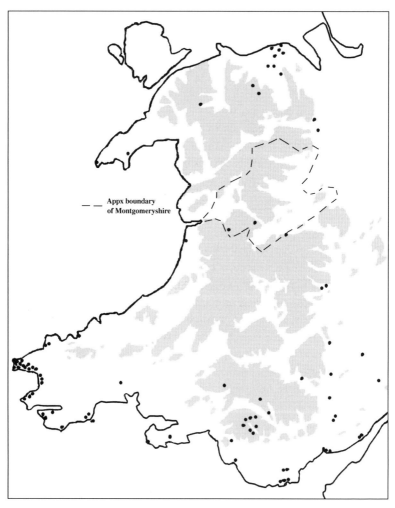

A map showing the distribution of later Mesolithic find spots across Wales, with clusters around St Davids, in the Glamorgan uplands and near Rhyl and Prestatyn in the north

The Mesolithic period is characterized by sweeping cultural transition. A distinct break separates Early Mesolithic from Late Mesolithic around 6700 BC, which roughly corresponds with the final insulation of Britain as an island (complete at around 6500 BC). Not only was Britain cut-off from Europe, but coastal plains and other lowland areas were lost under water, greatly diminishing exploitable land. Competition for resources became more intense and, as population grew, procurement systems necessarily became more complex. This could include exploitation of new environments, a change in hunting strategies and a change in technology, all of which are seen in the later Mesolithic. Earlier Mesolithic groups were highly mobile within an annual cycle, exploiting sizeable territories and integrating lowland and upland environments (Myers). Later Mesolithic groups remained mobile but to a lesser extent, and territorial range was reduced. The number of sites increases significantly, exploiting a greater range of environments, but the sites themselves are smaller. Territories appear to have more rigid boundaries. Later settlement patterns comprised a base residence from which forays were made by smaller groups during certain months of the year. These groups would then return to the base residence, usually during the winter season, to be assimilated back into the larger group. This is known as fissioning and fusioning, the dispersal and reuniting of groups such as is known in inland Inuit groups in northern Canada. It is an efficient pattern, making the best use of fewer available resources.

This cultural transition is associated with widespread changes in lithic technology (Myers). Regional styles in microlithic industry were developed and became prevalent, these style zones appearing to become more insulated and smaller in area over time (Myers). The long-distance raw material networks common in the open landscapes of the early Windermere Interstadial had disappeared and local raw materials were used almost exclusively, even if they were of poor quality (Lynch *et al*). Microliths appear in a wide variety of shapes including broad blades, triangle forms, tranchet adzes (woodworking), awls (hide-work), meche de foret (drill bit probably for beadwork), convex end-scrapers (hidework), burins (engraving), and a very few microdenticulates (little saws) (Lynch *et al*). The bow and arrow became very popular due to its efficiency in woodland hunting. Barbed antler and bone spearpoints continued to be used and antler mattocks were probably used for digging in soft, waterside sediments, perhaps for shellfish. The Late Mesolithic saw the introduction of narrow blade microliths. Lithic artefacts include platform cores, convex end-scrapers, pebble tools including limpet scoops or hammers, stone maceheads and ground stone axes.

For the first time, humans spread to the hills above 1,000 metres. Between 6000–3500 BC there is evidence that woodland fires were deliberately started. It's possible that Mesolithic communities were clearing forest to entice grazing animals, thus increasing their food procurement possibilities. Groups probably ranged within territories averaging 60–85 km in diameter. Although the raw material for lithics is primarily local, there is nevertheless evidence for transport of special items like the cowrie shells used for personal decoration found at King Arthur's Cave and Madawg rock shelter in the Wye Valley and the spotted mudstone beads found at Waun Fignen Felen, Breconshire.

In the late Mesolithic the uplands saw increased repeated but short-term visits associated with hunting.

Agriculture spread across Europe during this period, but the frontier appears to have been checked at the British borders at around 6000–5500 BC. There may have been sproadic, small scale cultivation, but a widespread adoption of agriculture is not thought to have taken hold in Britain until much later (Thomas), although this is still a matter of academic dispute. The British hunter-gatherers' low density of population did not necessitate a new subsistence strategy. Nevertheless their emphasis was on maintaining the food supply and this sometimes involved the use of domestic animals to offset crises. As the population increased, so came the need for greater food sources encouraging the slow spread of farming throughout Britain, a transition that would take thousands of years (Bradley, 1998). Status in these Late Mesolithic societies was still awarded to good hunters, shamen, craftsmen and those who could maintain large families.

The first evidence of human activity in Montgomeryshire appears during the Mesolithic. Earliest artefacts date from between 6000–5000 BC. The climate was wet and windy, with mild winters and warm summers. Woodlands included alder, oak, lime, birch and ash in the lowlands. Upland areas tend to have thinner soil and more rocks, so tree-cover is less dense and included hazel and pine in addition to lowland species (Arnold). Ten Mesolithic sites have so far been discovered in Montgomeryshire, primarily in the south and east of the county, the evidence taking the form of lithic scatters and stray finds—no settlement sites have yet been identified. This indicates that activity was probably limited to hunting parties and other short-term occupations. Upland sites are predominant, and all are located within five miles of a major river valley (the Severn to the east and the Dovey to the west). Two Tumps Barrow along the western end of the Kerry Hills has yielded a lithic assemblage which includes a geometric crescent. A surface collection from Caebetin Farm, a few miles to the west, includes convex scrapers

Distrubution of Mesolithic sites in Montgomeryshire,
showing a concentration around the River Severn
on the eastern side of the county

and edge-worked flakes of local origin. Two struck flints were recovered from a pond at Breidden. More flints have been discovered at Collfryn and Trelystan. As winters became milder and exploitation time was increasing—in the Pennines and Cleveland Hills sites are clustered either at over 1,200 feet or on the lowest ground, probably reflecting the annual migrations of red deer herds. In Montgomeryshire only three sites have been discovered below 1,000 feet above sea level: Clywedog (650 ft), Collfryn (320 ft) and Four Crosses (213 ft). An assemblage from Four Crosses includes small blades and a retouched flake. This site also provided a radiocarbon date from residual charcoal to the sixth millennium BC, and was probably a winter settlement spot due to its potential for winter grazing. Many, if not most of these find-spots, including Four Crosses, Breidden, Collfryn, Two Tumps, Ystrad Hynod and Trelystan, are sites of later occupation and cere-monial complexes. By the time this occurred, they may have been considered ancestral sites and of symbolic significance.

Gradually local communities were also developing funeral prac-tices. A nearly complete skeleton dated to 7100 +/-100 BC was discovered at Gough's Cave, Cheddar. A cemetery at Aveline's Hole in the Mendips was found to contain at least 80 burials dated from 7140 +/- 110 through to 6740 +/- 100 BC. Two skeletons found together were stained with ochre and accompanied by grave goods including a decorated portion of a horse incisor and the pierced teeth of red and giant deer, and pig (Lynch *et al*). Paviland Cave was found to contain one or two individuals dated to 7190 +/- 80 BP, but were not associated with any grave goods or other arte-facts. Worm's Head, Gower yielded early Mesolithic remains dated to 6800 BC. Late Mesolithic (6600–4800 BC) human remains were found at Ogof-yr-Ychen, Potter's Cave and Daylight Rock on Caldey; Foxhole, Gower; and Pontnewydd Cave, Denbighshire. These sites may represent deliberate deposits or burials, but not enough evidence remains to make an accurate interpretation. Beyond the burials themselves, several artefacts have been discov-ered which shed a little light on Mesolithic spirituality. Six engraved stones from Rhuddlan may provide evidence for ritual, though there is no way to determine whether these had symbolic significance. These pebbles were decorated with incised lines and patterns. One engraving could represent a house or basket, others look like leaves or reeds. Engraved stones were also discovered at Nab Head (Pembrokeshire) along with large numbers of beads. These were probably from burial jewelry (Lynch *et al*). A possible figurine was recovered from Nab Head as well; originally assessed to be a fake, it is currently being reassessed. Exotic spotted mudstone beads from Waun Fignen Felen (Breconshire) may have had symbolic or magical significance. A dozen pieces of red ochre were discovered at Prestatyn. Natural monoliths and other landscape features undoubtedly had significance to the Mesolithic people—the focus of a settlement at Gwernvale (Breconshire) was a spectacular natural monolith which was incorporated into a later megalithic tomb, reflecting its continued importance. The continued reverence for a sacred object or site is a common theme among prehistoric societies, as we shall see in the Neolithic and Bronze Age megalithic cultures.

The Neolithic
The earlier Neolithic spanned from 4,400 BC through to 2,900 BC. Britain was still suffering land loss to the western peninsulae as a result of post-glacial rising sea levels. The climate was warm and wet for the most part, but varied throughout regions. On the western peninsulae of Wales—Pembrokeshire, Lleyn and Anglesey—the mild winters and sparse tree cover allowed longer growing seasons and therefore attracted the densest settlement of the time, Anglesey containing one of the richest groups of Neolithic monuments in Europe. Deciduous woodlands covered the landscape, although the forests were moving past their prime by the end of this period. Valleys were probably densely wooded, with the tree line at 600 metres. Birch and oak appeared throughout Wales, with the southwest dominated by hazel, the north by alder, and oak and lime dominating in mid-Wales. Pine and elm were rare. The reason behind the widespread decline of elm is the source of controversy—there is speculation about human interference through farming, but elm disease or infestation could also account for the decimation. Animal species remained much the same as during the Mesolithic with the exception of red deer whose population may have declined due to hunting.

The early Neolithic saw changes throughout the world, one of the most important developments being the advent of writing. Script probably began as early symbolism on religious art dating to 7,000 BC, and cuneiform writing had been developed in Mesopotamia by 3100. The practice of embalming the dead began around 3400 BC. In 3450 BC, the world's first cities appeared along the banks of the Tigris and Euphrates rivers, and the area saw the development of a lunar calendar, metalworking and medicine. By 3300 BC the Aegean world begins to be populated. Sumeria was founded by 3200 BC—the 'Dawn of History'—and there is evidence of wheeled transportation.

Shamanism and magic were being practiced by many cultures during the early Neolithic. In the Mediterranean, various peoples were developing complex systems involving astrology, numerology, pantheons, divination and magical spells complete with props and magical language. These disciplines would later develop into the world's first sciences, medicine and mathematics. The Tassili cave paintings clearly depict a shamanic figure with mushrooms sprouting from his/her body indicating religious use of these powerful hallucinogens.

Distilled spirits and beer were introduced, probably by 4000 BC in Mesopotamia. Needless to say, it quickly spread throughout Europe and Asia. Opium was cultivated in Europe by 6000 BC and there is evidence for its use throughout the continent. Cannabis was in use by the third millennium BC throughout Asia, where it was used by magicians and Taoists and the practice spread throughout Europe.

Neolithic people in Britain probably practiced a form of 'tethered mobility', returning periodically, movements probably being seasonal, to a number of fixed points within a given territory (Thomas). Small groups sharing common traditions interacted with one another, forming a broader, regional group, seven or eight of which have been identified as covering Britain in this period. The construction of tombs was common among most groups (Darvill) although some areas in Central Wales, including Montgomeryshire, and the north-east are devoid of tombs. It's difficult to tell if these areas were uninhabited or if they simply supported a non-tomb building population. During the earlier Neolithic the Welsh population, which probably now numbered around 2,300 individuals, was scattered around the coasts and lowlands. As the population grew, people moved up the valleys and into the uplands. There is still some evidence that suggests the continued use of caves throughout the period, although this is minimal. There is no evidence of grouped or enclosed settlements from the early Neolithic. Just six sites have yielded postholes, pits, sherds and hearths, and three have yielded some structural evidence, the most impressive being Clegyr Boia, Pembrokeshire, which is located on a rocky summit and comprises an unenclosed 0.25 hectares (Lynch *at al*). The apparent domestic structures therefore appear singly and widely dispersed on the landscape, albeit that each is large enough to provide for an extended family.

The majority of evidence for human activity in Neolithic Montgomeryshire comes from the eastern and southern areas of the

Distrubution of Neolithic sites in Montgomeryshire. Whilst there is still a concentration of sites around the River Severn, people are clearly moving into the uplands too

county, particularly in the Severn Valley. Only the finds from beneath the Bronze Age barrow at Ysgwennant, Llansilin suggest penetration deep into the side valleys. The earliest permanent residents of the upper Severn Valley probably came from the Midlands Plain via the Breidden/Llanymynech gap in the early fourth millennium BC. This area is the confluence of the Tanat, Vyrnwy and Severn Rivers, which would have been used as routes to the interior. This may have been an important social gathering spot, perhaps the site of fairs or markets. Certainly, large barrows and ring ditches have been discovered in close proximity to this site suggesting cultural importance (Gibson, 2002). Toward the middle Neolithic, populations expanded up the valleys. Sites include Ffridd Faldwyn, Montgomery (where Peterborough Ware was found) and Trelystan on Long Mountain (Grooved Ware). Decorated pottery known as Peterborough Ware first began to appear in South Wales during the Middle Neolithic (Lynch *et al*) and in use in the Severn Valley by the early third millennium BC (Gibson, 2002).

Funerary and temporary settlement sites have yielded a variety of artefacts including clusters of polished stone axes, pottery, flintwork, leaf-shaped arrowheads and, at Newtown and Llanwddyn, polished chisels and stone maceheads. Llanwddyn is also the site of the only known megalithic tombs in Montgomeryshire (see below). Polished stone axes have also been found at some upland and hilltop sites including Breidden, Ffridd Faldwyn and Cefn Carnedd (the latter two probably being temporary settlement sites). Several clusters of polished stone axes have been found to the west of Newtown particularly at Machynllech, Breidden, Carno and Caersws. Clusters of these axes usually indicate settlement locations while casual finds of flintwork such as those found on the Kerry Hills above Dolfor indicate a travel route or short-term hunting camp (Arnold).

By 4500 BC most of Europe was practising agriculture except for Britain and parts of northern Europe (Bradley, 1998). The absence of clear evidence for widespread, sustained cultivation and permanent substantial domestic architecture suggests that agriculture did not take a firm hold in Britain until well past this period, perhaps as late as the middle Bronze Age (Thomas). There is evidence, however, for small-scale horticulture, plots being planted

Polished flint axe found in Breconshire

in various locations as the group moved around, the produce being harvested on returning later in the year (Thomas). In addition to this small-scale gardening it appears that animal husbandry, notably of cattle, sheep and pigs, was probably initiated during the later Mesolithic. Traces of hunting camps show the continued importance of wild game as a food source. At Moel-y-Gaer, Clwyd the remains of a wooden windbreak surrounded by flint waste dating to 2994+/-40 BC suggests a temporary hunting stand (Darvill).

One of the most prevalent artefacts of the Neolithic period is the polished stone axe. By the Middle Neolithic, the axe was being exchanged across distant regions and was invested with symbolic roles in addition to its practical use. The raw materials for this widely distributed tool came from five rock sources in Wales, two in the north and three in the Preseli Mountains in the south-west. Graig Lwyd at Penmaenmawr (Caernarfonshire) is the best-known axe factory. These axes may have been formally traded by a merchant class or simply passed among neighbouring groups (Lynch *et al*).

Flint continued to be worked in Britain through the third millennium BC, but flint implements and other personal goods of the early Neolithic are neither common nor distinctive. In Wales, the only small flint artefact that can be confidently ascribed to this time is the leaf–shaped arrowhead reflecting the continuing importance of hunting (Lynch *et al*, 59). Flint mining was taking place at Grimes Graves, Norfolk, but wouldn't reach its peak until 2100 BC. A fascinating aspect of the industry is revealed by a shrine located in a small chamber of the mine comprising a carved statuette of a pregnant woman surrounded by chalk stones, flint blocks and antler picks. This further evidences a connection between industrial / domestic and religious spheres. Flint was also being quarried on a large scale at five major locations, two in the north and three in the Preseli Mountains.

Specialized industrial activities included boneworking, wood-working, ceramics and boatmaking. The Somerset levels yielded bowls, pins, figurines, boat paddles, long bows, arrowshafts and a mallet from the third millennium (Darvill). A possible flute made of perforated sheep bone was found in the tomb at Penywyrlod (Breconshire) and enigmatic stone discs, similar to those found in burial chambers of Britain and Brittany were found at Pant y Saer (Anglesey), Ty Isaf (Breconshire) and Penywyrlod. There is very little evidence of personal decoration (Lynch).

Neolithic pottery is found in both ritual and domestic contexts in Wales and comprises undecorated, shallow round-bottomed bowls and some cups. Pottery was made at domestic settlement sites with local materials, dramatically altering the lives of Neolithic people allowing for the storage, mixing and cooking of food. Not only did they transform food production, they impacted the rhythms of social life. Pots were imbued with symbolic meaning and were used in ceremonial contexts, usually transformed by being deliberately broken—this is determined by closely examining wear patterns, the context of the deposition and surrounding evidence. The largest assemblage of Neolithic Welsh pottery was found beneath the Gwernvale cairn (Breconshire) and was dated to 3900 BC.

Skeletal analysis reveals that the people were small, between 1.5-1.65 metres tall, with well-developed muscle channels, flat-tened shin bones (from squatting), prominent brow ridges and muscular jaws. The only pronounced difference from present-day humans is an edge-to-edge bite (as opposed to front to back) more similar to the Mesolithic inhabitants of the area. Diseases were common, especially arthritis. Almost every individual over 25 exhibited some signs of the disease particularly on the hands and feet. Teeth were generally in bad condition. The Pant y Saer tomb in Anglesey yielded nine full-term fetuses testifying to the risks of childbirth (Lynch *et al*). In all, life expectancy was probably around 30 years, though 50-year-old individuals have been found (Darvill).

In all facets of domestic life, the importance of the group is stressed over the importance of the individual. The erection of megalithic tombs is evidence of this. Communal projects of this magnitude require a population with a common purpose and within which conformity is valued above individuality. A religion guaranteeing success if followed faithfully, and threatening displeasure of the gods or ancestors on the whole group when this is not the case is an effective mode of governing such a population. An elder or priest who has knowledge of rituals and taboos would be the dominating force. Ostracism would have been an extremely effective method of punishment among people who depended on the group for their daily survival.

The importance of the group over the individual as well as their seasonal cycle of circulation are reflected in ceremonial practices. Spectacular megalithic tombs began to appear during this time, presumably reflecting settlement patterns as they must have been erected in close proximity to sites of yearly population aggregation. These grand structures required an enormous investment of time and energy, and are dedicated to the commemoration of a group rather than one important individual. Within the tombs are the bones of women, men and children reflecting no hierarchy of age or gender. These bones were disarticulated (taken apart) and defleshed (stripped of flesh by exposure or animal activity), and the remains more than likely circulated among several mortuary structures in various ceremonies before being placed together in the tomb. Thus the identity and status of each individual is stripped, leaving a group of anonymous ancestors. Circulation is a recurring theme in Neolithic culture and is reflected in settlement patterns, mortuary practices described above, the circulation of gifts between related groups and communities, even in the cycle of the extraction of raw materials, such as clay, its transformation into pots, subsequent use, and then their breakage and deposition in the monuments. The circulation of bones leads archaeologists to believe that these tombs represent places of transition rather than funerary monuments, or 'final resting places' as we think of tombs today.

As the Neolithic period progressed towards the Bronze Age, there is more evidence of a material culture. Communities generally remained mobile, with movements appearing to be more opportunistic rather than cyclic in nature. Territorality remained in effect. A growing interest in status occurred during this later period, evidenced by the increasing practice of individual burials with grave goods, a tradition thought to originate in Yorkshire. Communal tombs were abandoned in southern England and eventually in Wales as well. This transition occurred early in the Severn Valley, including Montgomeryshire, before spreading throughout Wales. Montgomeryshire's location directly bordering southern England meant that new practices often appeared there prior to their adoption throughout the rest of Wales.

Four Crosses at Welshpool is a large mortuary and ceremonial complex that was built over millennia. At the centre of a vast burial pit is one of the earliest features, a barrow of the type normally constructed in the Bronze Age. This barrow contained three individual inhumations, one of which was accompanied by an exotic vessel. Radiocarbon dates suggest a time of construction between 3200 and 3100 BC, still within the time span termed 'Neolithic'. A single inhumation found at the Trelystan complex, also in Montgomeryshire, yielded the same date (Britnell 1982, 136).

Deposition of objects is found at almost all Neolithic ceremonial monuments and burial sites in Britain. Initially objects were placed in the ground, usually in the pits, ditches and/or post holes of monuments as part of ceremonial activity. Items deposited usually consisted of domestic tools, human and animal bones, stone and flintwork, and were often broken or burnt, ritualizing their transition from household item to votive item. Towards the end of the Neolithic the deposition itself was a ceremonial event and became more and more common in graves, although items deposited remained much the same. Some human remains were found not at ceremonial centres or tombs, but at settlement sites and specialized enclosures (Bradley, 1998). Not all sites yielding human bones, therefore, can be classified as tombs, but may have been places of transition, part of a larger circuit of sites hosting the relic, perhaps representing a rite of passage and reflecting the circulation of people in their migrations through the landscape. Skulls and skull fragments appeared to be of highest value, for they are found in a myriad of settings including 'pit deposits, buried land surfaces, causewayed enclosure ditches, river sediments and the post-holes of monumental structures' (Thomas, Pp 226).

The placing of mundane items in the earth may have been a means of exerting influence or of sanctifying or transforming a place, the sacred place itself being considered to be a permeable borderland between the mundane world and the world of the spirits and ancestors. The community would have enhanced the relationship between these worlds by placing everyday items at the borderland between them. Depositions at ceremonial monuments were generally placed in the walls of the structure via post-holes and especially at entrances and exits, further enhancing the notion of borders.

Barrows and Long Mounds
In some places, the dead were left to decay inside their houses. As this practice went out of favour, long mounds of similar proportions to the houses were built in proximity to the settlement and with the same alignments as the houses. Earthen long mounds or barrows are a distinctive feature of the earlier Neolithic from around 4000–3500 BC. Their similarity in shape, alignment, entrance position and internal organization to longhouses has led some to believe that they are symbolically related, perhaps representing the house of the dead. In addition, the tombs are very often found in 'communities' reflecting the communities of the living.

Three long barrows have been found in Montgomeryshire, two at Berriew and one at Churchstoke. The latter, the New House Long Barrow, overlooks the Cambrian mountains and the Severn Valley. Aligned south-west/north-east, the mound, measuring 30 metres by 18 metres and oval-shaped, has its broader, higher end toward the south-west. This is unusual as most barrows are aligned with the broader end towards the east. Possible kerbstones were discovered at the north-east perimeter (Gibson 2002). Lower Luggy long barrow, dated to between 3700 and 3300 BC, is possibly the earliest monument of the later Dyffryn Lane henge complex. This classic barrow is trapezoidal in shape, perhaps echoing the style of Cotswold-Severn group of tombs (see below), with a wooden fenced forecourt and surrounded by a wooden palisade. The burial area itself is covered by boulders. The second of the Berriew barrows is found in the same field, is oval-shaped and shorter at 40 metres by 30 metres wide. In addition two square barrows have been found close to the longer trapezoidal barrow.

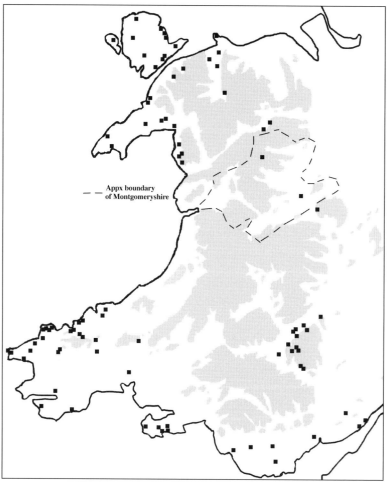

Distribution map of Neolithic tombs across Wales,
showing concentrations around Anglesey and the north coast, the
south-west, Gower and the Black Mountains

Causewayed enclosures

Ambiguous, mainly circular enclosures constructed of banks and ditches and usually punctuated with causeways or entrances began to appear on the British landscape during the earlier Neolithic. There are over 50 examples across Britain of these features of all sizes and scales occurring in a variety of locations including hilltops and promontories, hill slopes and valley floors (Darvill). These have been interpreted in many ways, including as settlements, cattle pens, ritual monuments and public gathering places for exchange. There is often evidence of feasting at these and later incarnations of this monument type, and this leads to the assumption that the enclosure emphasized a function or significance already inherent in the area. Some of these enclosures surrounded or were surrounded by houses/structures, yet others were on the periphery of a settlement. Carn Brea in Cornwall was dated to before 3000 BC, has a wall up to 2 metres thick and required approximately 30,000 man-hours to build. Crickley Hill in Gloucestershire straddles the border between two very different environments—the rich Severn Vale to the west and dramatic Cotswold uplands to the east. Similar environmental contrasts surrounding these and other enclosures is probably significant. In addition, such enclosures are regularly found in pairs or as part of a complex of sites (Darvill). Later in the Neolithic defensive ramparts were erected around some of the enclosures and the entrances blocked. Several impressive examples of causewayed enclosures can be found in Montgomeryshire. Ffrydd Faldwyn near Montgomery and Cefn Carnedd near Llandinam may be causewayed enclosures (Arnold). At the former, Early Neolithic pottery sherds, similar to those recovered at Breidden, a polished axe flake and flintwork including an arrowhead, flakes and a scraper may be part of a ritual deposition in one of the enclosure ditches. The ritual complexes at Sarn-y-bryn-caled/Coed-y-dinas, Trelystan and Four Crosses all contain evidence of these early monuments as well as later types.

Chambered Tombs

Perhaps the most spectacular edifices of Neolithic architecture are the chambered tombs. Most of these survive stripped of their covering cairn so all that remains is the inner chamber consisting of upright stones supporting a large capstone. There are many variations of the chambered tomb, the more recognized, distinctive types in Wales including the Cotswold-Severn tradition originating in Breconshire and the Bristol Channel region, Portal Dolmens with several regionally dominant groups and Passage Graves with connections to the Irish Sea province and Atlantic Europe.

Cotswold-Severn tombs comprise chambers set within trapezoidal, neatly walled cairns and were built in locations that already had significance (Thomas). The chambers were located at various places in the cairn and remained accessible after construction and deposition. Inhumations consisted of disarticulated unburnt bone. The design was influenced by earthen long barrow mounds and at least two additional traditions of continental chamber architecture. Groups building these tombs in stone and wood were in close proximity to each other as proved by the recent discovery of the Lower Luggy earthen long barrows near Welshpool dated to 3700–3300 BC (Lynch *et al*).

Portal Dolmens are a widespread family of monuments occurring alongside other tombs throughout western Wales and north Pembrokeshire. The monument consists of a simple, box-shaped burial chamber either covered with a cairn or set into the landscape. The classic Portal Dolmen form is a tall portal leading to a single rectangular chamber covered by a magnificent capstone. A forecourt at the entrance, some of which were added later, is fairly common. The chambers were usually covered by a small round or long cairn which for the most part, since these tombs were often located on lower slopes and subjected to greater agricultural and pastoral activity, have long since disappeared.

Passage graves consist of a forecourt, an entrance portal of orthostats and a lintel leading to a passage

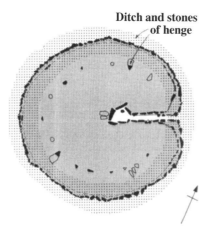

Ditch and stones of henge

Bryn Celli Ddu, Anglesey— an example of a later passage grave

34

which then opens into a chamber. Some tombs have additional chambers accessed via the passage. This type of monument appeared in the Late Neolithic and Early Bronze Age. Only seven early monuments survive, all located in western Wales and Anglesey, later types being found in northern Wales. These graves are influenced by Irish tradition and are the only monuments of this era to be decorated.

In Montgomeryshire there are only two possible surviving examples of chambered tombs: Afon y Dolou Gwynion and Ciddig, both in Llanwddyn. Interpretations of both these monuments as chambered tombs are suspect due to their poor condition and lack of similar structures in the area. Afon y Dolou, of the two structures more probably a true chambered tomb and most resembling a portal dolmen, is located on a spur of the highest peak in the area. With the high peak rising behind to the north, the structure looks out over distant mountains to the south, west and east and a small valley directly below to the south and west. The surrounding landscape gives one the impression of being on a dome rising up from the valley floor at the centre of a large circle of mountains. (This impression is common to almost every site I visited in Montgomeryshire.) The chamber is rectangular and measures 5 by 2.5 metres. Three standing stones on the north-east side are a possible constricted entrance measuring 1.5 metres long by 6 metres wide. A low bank surrounds the chamber, possibly the

Bryn yr Hen Bobl, Anglesey

result of digging through the covering mound. There are no capstones on the site and the area is much disturbed by modern activity, even though it is somewhat remote. Ciddig barrow, located nearby, is a circular cairn probably related to a portal dolmen style that has suffered much disturbance including robbing. Evidence of former kerbing is present, and a 'tail' of stone extends from the central mound out to the south-west. This may have been deliberately added or the result of damage, but is similar to one at Bryn yr Hen Bobl, Anglesey, and is evidence for a Neolithic construction date (Gibson, 2002).

Continuity of Sacred Landscape/Complexes
One of the most interesting phenomena of the Neolithic is the appearance of ritual complexes, as religious and burial structures were built on ground that was already considered sacred due to the presence of older monuments. The significance of these older monuments could be traced even further back to ancestral settlement sites and important gathering places along ancient migration routes. (Many early Neolithic and Mesolithic sites have been discovered purely by chance due to the excavation of a later site laying atop the earlier evidence.) This practice led to the construction of ritual complexes comprising many monuments built and modified over a period of thousands of years and spanning from the early Neolithic right through to the Bronze Age. The earliest constructions in these complexes tend to be of labour intensive, grand earthworks such as pit circles, ring ditches, causewayed enclosures, henges and cursuses embellished with timber circles, later replaced by stone circles. These were often built around existing barrows. Later monuments would include cairns, tombs, standing stones and stone circles. Each new generation would have a different relationship with the monuments, rebuilding and modifying them to suit the changing belief system.

Montgomeryshire boasts several ritual complexes with their earliest constructions dating from the early to middle Neolithic.

The lowland site of Four Crosses, Berriew, in eastern Montgomeryshire was in use between 3200 and 1800 BC. The earliest phase comprises a large pit grave or round barrow surrounded by a ring ditch. A single inhumation of a crouched adult was found in the pit accompanied by an early Neolithic Welsh undecorated round-bottomed ceramic bowl, a calf's jaw-bone and an unusually shaped stone. Oak charcoal was discovered in the pit and may be associated with burnt areas outside suggesting a ceremony or ritual feast. Stains on the ground are thought to be the residue from two adolescents or adults whose legs may have have been disarticulated and removed. Exotic Peterborough Ware sherds were deposited in the surrounding ring ditch. A scraper and two chisel arrowheads were the only flintwork found in the barrows excavated at Four Crosses, but the arrowheads may prove to be from a later deposition as the round barrow and ring ditch were enlarged in several stages until the Bronze Age. It forms part of a dispersed cemetery revealed by aerial photography.

Trelystan, a long lived ritual complex dating from the late Neolithic to early Bronze Age, is located on Long Mountain in eastern Montgomeryshire. An early burial dated to 3100 BC consisted of a mature adult female in a wooden coffin or chamber covered by a stone cairn. She was accompanied by a cremation burial containing only a tooth. This burial was not associated with any pottery. The next phase included a number of pits, including a pit grave. A later phase consisted of a pair of barrows, probably a family cemetery, dated between 2100 and 1800 BC. At the beginning of this later phase, each burial was placed beneath its own separate mound and some were accompanied by small food vessels. The final phase of burials were urned cremations inserted into the earlier mounds. Many of these urns were deposited upside down.

The development of Sarn-y-bryn-caled, Montgomeryshire, spanned almost 2000 years, from the late Neolithic to Early Bronze age. The initial monument was a rectangular cursus 10 metres wide by 400 metres long, dating to 3930 BC (Gibson, 1992a). The cursus is aligned north-east / south-west and comprised two parallel ditches with a number of causeways. Modification of the cursus continued until 2695 BC. Five ring ditches, 10 to 35 metres in diameter, possibly represent damaged late Neolithic to early Bronze Age barrows. A horse-shoe shaped element, 8 metres in diameter with a pair of timber posts possibly forming a lintelled entranceway was then added, and is associated with four cremation burials and Peterborough Ware. A timber circle comprising 20 enormous posts with an inner circle of six posts, was added in the early Bronze Age, around 2100 BC, and surrounds the central feature of the monument: a central pit shaped like an inverted pyramid and containing two cremation burials. Both were originally contained in a bag or basket, one of which also held four prestigious barbed and tanged flint arrowheads which appear to have been lodged in the individual's body, suggesting a possible human sacrifice. A small food vessel vase with possible food residue on the inner surface was recovered with the cremation. To the east of the inner circle, a timber structure was located, its size and shape suggesting an altar-like structure. The latest phase of the complex comprised two ring-ditches at nearby Coed-y-Dinas. Beaker pottery dated to 2000 BC was found at this site (Gibson, 1992a).

Dyffryn Lane, Berriew, again in the Severn Valley south of Welshpool centres around the 60 metres in diameter Dyffryn Lane Henge that itself surrounds a central barrow. There is evidence for a kerb or stone circle and a nearby standing stone known as Maen Bueno may have been part of the complex. Twelve ring ditches, two round barrows, a standing stone and a ritual pit were added later. Lower Luggy long barrow lies 550 metres north-west of the henge, and is probably the earliest feature of the complex, dating from between 3700 and 3300 BC. There are two square barrows and a round barrow in the area of Lower Luggy dating from approximately the same time (Gibson, 2002).

Dyffryn Lane, Berriew and Sarn-y-bryn-caled near Welshpool form part of a linear arrangement of monuments along the valley floor, possibly relating to the profile of the nearby Breidden mountains. There is evidence of a further timber circle and burial monuments on the Tanat Valley floor at Meusydd. Excavations of the Llandegai Complex (Caernarfonshire), a large, inland ritual complex dating from the early Neolithic through the Bronze Age, revealed two large henges. The first has a single entrance and is associated with axe trading. The other has two entrances and yielded unusual deposits of stone and Beaker pottery. A cursus monument runs west from between the henges toward a small hengiform monument in the Ogwen Valley, whilst Bronze Age burials have been found clustered around the main Neolithic sanctuary. Excavations beneath the second henge revealed earlier post-holes suggesting a 6 by 13 metre timber structure identified at first as an Early Neolithic house (Lynch *et al*, 131). An external hearth, pits and domestic debris were found scattered outside the structure. Some believe the structure to be cermonial in nature, given the scarcity of domestic evidence from that time.

Renewed interest in larger monuments appears to have occurred around 2000 BC, when major construction at Trelystan, Four Crosses and Sarn-y-bryn-caled took place.

These groupings may be ritual foci, or may reflect a proliferation of monuments across the landscape, many of which have been lost or are yet to be discovered (Gibson, 2002).

Late Neolithic

The late Neolithic spans from around 2,900 to 2,300 BC. During this time, the Sumerian King, Gilgamesh was ruling the city of Uruk with more than 50,000 subjects. Nearby Egypt was fast becoming an enormous empire; the first pyramid was built in 2700 BC, the second in 2560 BC, and the Sphinx in 2500 BC.

In Britain the climate was still favourable but gradually declining from the optimal conditions of recent periods — winters were becoming more severe and the summers cooler and drier. This meant that the uplands were only becoming attractive for grazing and exploitation during the summer months and settlement remained concentrated in the valleys. Analysis of flint tools determined that meat processing became more important during the Late Neolithic, but it is still difficult to demonstrate a widespread pastoral economy due to the absence of permanent settlement and animal evidence (Lynch *et al*). Arable activity was probably on the increase as evidenced by pollen analysis, but there is no evidence that farming was the dominant economy as yet. Cattle and sheep were present in some numbers as were red deer as evidenced by the antler tools used by miners. Tree cover was fairly thin and ranged to 600 metres, with oak, ash and birch as the dominant species. Pollen evidence of deforestation becomes more prevalent in the uplands after around 2500 BC, indicating possible human interference. Plateaux and ridges were bare.

Many circular structures dating to the late Neolithic have been discovered, measuring approximately 4 metres in diameter with hearths taking up most of the floor, so leaving little room for indoor working. These sites generally yield pottery sherds, flint tools and small pits with domestic refuse, and were presumably small, domestic structures, used rather sporadically.

Contact with England and Ireland was maintained throughout the late Neolithic, revealing its influences in trade and exchange goods as well as funereal and ceremonial practices (Lynch *et al*). The crafting of metal reached Britain by around 2500 BC, the first metal products being valued as ceremonial or status items. The Irish became expert metalsmiths, presumably deriving their knowledge from continental Europe where metallurgy began much earlier. Most early Welsh metal products derive from a single Irish source. However, the Welsh industry soon began to expand. Meanwhile, Welsh polished axeheads were much in demand and the trade was booming. Penmaenmawr and Preseli were important sources for bluestone, although Preseli stone wasn't particularly attractive or blue as a polished stone, suggesting that Preseli stone had different, perhaps sacred attributes that accounted for its popularity. Weapons such as battle-axes and mace-heads continued to be made from stone deliberately chosen for its colour and texture. In particular, the elegant ovoid mace-heads from north-eastern Wales were sought after as status items, as attested by their presence in several individual graves in Yorkshire. Interestingly, they are absent from northern Welsh graves, perhaps due to being too local in design and therefore ownership providing no prestige. Flintworking declined in the Late Neolithic and appears to cease before the advent of the Bronze Age, but exotic amber and Faience continued to be imported.

Personal decoration began to appear to be more in demand around this time, reflecting the growing importance of individuals and status derived from religious power, wealth acquisition and/or lineage. This is an effect of increasing sedentarism, for when a culture begins to settle in permanent houses there is room for the accumulation of material goods. The status that once belonged to the greatest hunter/provider and craftspeople began to shift to those who could acquire the most surplus.

Peterborough Ware continues to be found. The only apparent Welsh variant on the style is bird-bone decoration. Peterborough

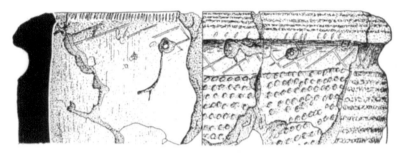

An example of Peterborough Ware found at Sarn-y-bryn-caled

Ware can be divided into several subtypes including Ebbsfleet ware, Mortlake ware and Fengate ware. Ebbsfleet ware, from the Ebbsfleet Valley in north-east Kent, is usually well made with a globular shape. Simple rims, distinct necks, rounded or sometimes sharp shoulders also characterize the ware. Moderate decoration appears around the upper part of the neck, at times extending over the rim to the inside of the vessel, the decoration comprising incised fingernail and cord impressions and pits in the neck made with the fingertip. Mortlake ware developed from Ebbsfleet ware, but is generally not as well-made as its predecessor, and is of thicker and softer fabric. Usually with round bases (although some flat bases have been found), the rims are heavy and projecting with deeply hollowed necks and sharp shoulders. The impressed decorations are made with fingers or bird or other bone, and is usually a herring-bone motif covering the better part of the exterior and upper part of the interior of the vessels. Cord impressions and a new technique known as rustication (pinching the clay between two fingernails) are also common decorative motifs. The neck-pits common to Ebbsfleet ware were still occasionally used. Fengate ware is the final stage in the Peterborough sequence. In this the vessels are straight-sided with flattened bases. Rims are T-shaped or collared, projecting over the edges. All three types—Ebbsfleet, Mortlake and Fengate—are used from 3400 to 2500 BC (Gibson & Kinnes 1997).

The less common Grooved Ware was discovered at Trelystan dating between 28-2400 BC, Sarn-y-bryn-caled, Walton, and on the isle of Anglesey. Contemporary with later Peterborough wares and Beakers, Grooved ware probably originated on Orkney, developing from earlier Unstan ware. The style spread all over the British Isles

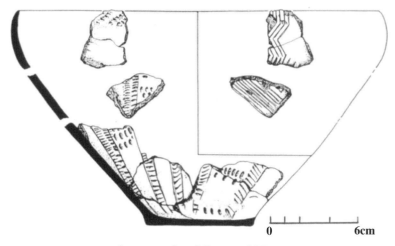

An example of Grooved Ware,
this one found at Walton, Radnorshire

by the early third millennium BC, and is present at the first level of
Stonehenge. The vessels are usually flat bottomed with straight
sides sloping outwards. Grooved, incised, dotted and applied decoration appears around the rims, although later Grooved Ware has
many different varieties with complex and applied decorations.The
applique decorations may have derived from wicker basketry.
Many Grooved Ware pots are found at henge sites and burials.
Some vessels from the Balfarg/Balbirnie Neolithic ritual complex
in Ireland have been found to contain remnants of black henbane
(*Hyoscyamus niger*). This herb is an hallucinogen which may have
ritual significance (Long, *et al.*). Beaker sherds have been discovered in tombs that clearly antedate the pottery, suggesting continued
ceremony at these old monuments. New burials included
Peterborough and Grooved Ware predominantly. These two wares
were seldom intermixed, but appear in the same types of settlements in Wales between 3400 and 2400 BC.

Beaker vessels are a finely made, reddish pottery initially
imported from the Rhineland by 2600 BC and subsequently manufactured in Britain. Seven style phases are recognized, spanning
1,000 years of production. Although Beakers were used in domestic
settings, they are most commonly found in single inhumation

contexts. Beakers are rare in Wales, with just 40 examples found, and then only in later styles dating to after 2500 BC. At the appearance of Beakers, ceremonial and funereal practice underwent some dramatic changes. Single inhumation burials often accompanied by beautiful grave goods became the accepted practice, with the body (of men, women and children) usually buried in a crouched position. Large public monuments also began to appear, including henges, circles and rows, though whether this was due to the influence of the 'Beaker Folk', or is unconnected is subject to debate. It was once thought that Beaker Folk invaded Britain, bringing new customs with them, but there is no evidence of social upheaval at this time and it is now generally accepted that the material culture was adopted due to the interest in exotica. Other items introduced at this time include flat axes made of Irish copper, copper daggers and knives, jet beads and buttons, copper awls and pins, and gold objects. Montgomeryshire sites yielding Beaker sherds include Collfryn Enclosure, Four Crosses, Llandegai henge, Elmtree, Trelystan and the Breidden. Beaker ware continued to be used in domestic settings and (mostly) single inhumation graves until at least 1700 BC (Lynch *et al*).

Examples of beakers from across Wales. That top left was found at Aberbechan, that top right at Darowen, both in Montgomeryshire. Those on the bottom row come from across Wales and are dated to a period between the two examples from Montgomeryshire

Although abandoned in England, communal burial practice in Wales continued until the Late Neolithic as evidenced by pottery from this date found inside tombs. As mentioned above, a barrow at Four Crosses is dated 3200 BC and is of a type normally dated to the early Bronze Age (2,300BC). Trelystan yields a single inhumation of the same date in the Middle Neolithic (Britnell 1982, 136). Single inhumations weren't to gain popularity until much later, however, starting in the south of the country and spreading north at the appearance of the Long Necked Beaker, the final Beaker phase. Some of these burials are cremations (which took over as the dominant practice by around 2000 BC), some are unburnt and there are a few multiple burials tucked in. There is no evidence of political or social upheaval nor of conflict at this time, so the people were simply adapting gradually to new practices. Beginning at around the same time, the practice of using a single mound for multiple individual inhumations, a sort of cemetery, each accompanied by grave goods, became the norm (Lynch *et al*). This practice continued until at least 1000 BC.

Henge monuments are the best known but most enigmatic of the Late Neolithic ceremonial monuments. A henge is a circular ceremonial area enclosed by a bank and an outer ditch, punctuated by one or more causeways entering the central space. Henges elaborate the distinction between the outside and the inside of the circle as represented in the earlier causewayed enclosures and introduced a greater complexity of classification of space and material objects. Many were a part of a larger group of monuments that were in use for hundreds and sometimes thousands of years. Renewal and modification continued almost constantly throughout the period of use, involving an enormous investment of time and energy. The circular shape of the henge as constructed by the bank and ditch was often enhanced and modified with timber or pit circles, and eventually stone circles by around 2500 BC. Forty timber circles have been recognized so far in Britain, ranging from central Scotland to south-west England and a variation in central Ireland. Entrances and exits were sometimes lined with posts of timber or stone, whilst circles or spirals within circles, platforms and kerbs were constructed. All of these elements served to direct the flow of people in and around the monument, as well as to direct their visual experience of the monument in relation to the world surrounding it. Members of the local community may have stood on the bank to watch the ceremonies taking place within the circle. Objects have often been found deposited in the ditches and banks, suggesting ritual use. Burial was not the primary function of henges, though some may have been so used later in their life.

Linear monuments such as an avenue or cursus of stone or timber were sometimes constructed to lead to or around the henges or connect them with surrounding monuments in the case of the larger complexes comprising several features. At the same time interest in celestial phenomena increased and henges were built/modified to be astronomically aligned to certain stars, the sun and moon, or fixed cardinal points. Solar alignments have been demonstrated at Woodhenge and possibly at Sarn-y-bryn-caled (Gibson, 1993). A timber circle found at Caebatin Hill, Kerry comprised a small oval circle of stakes, covered by round barrow.

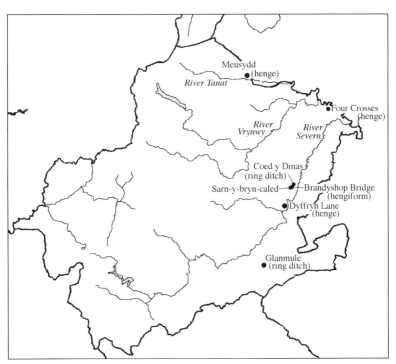

Map showing the location of hengiform sites in Montgomeryshire

The circle was oriented to the cardinal points with larger posts to the east and west and an edge-set stone at the south (Gibson, 2002).

It is possible that these monuments originally existed on a neutral zone at the borders of cultural regions, providing a safe place for the exchange of goods. Subsequently, the processing of human remains, which involved the practices of exposure, defleshing and disarticulation prior to circulation of the final relics, became a central occupation at these enclosures, identified through the discovery of chemical residue in the soils, especially phosphates, left as a result of this activity. Thus control of an enclosure meant control both of the borderlands between living cultural groups and between the living and the dead. These seasonal events of gathering, exchange and ritual would increase the prestige and power of the controlling groups (Thomas).

The henges often incorporated one or more barrows or other types of tomb either within the circle or in direct proximity and intervisible with it. Landmarks of cultural importance were often visible from the henges, such as distant mountains that may have ancestral significance. This tie to the past—the dead and the ancestral homeland—remains a central part of the monument's significance. Over time, the monument served to validate the community's ancestral/mythical ties to the place.

Henges can range from 60 metres in diameter to 14 metres (mini-henges) and always occur in conjunction with other Neolithic and early Bronze Age monuments. They may have been lintelled, as at Stonehenge with its mortice and tenon tongue-and-groove joints that may have been in imitation of earlier timber circles.

Eight henge sites are recognised in the Severn Valley, all located on low-lying ground on river gravels and include Sarn-y-bryn-caled, Meusydd, Dyffryn Lane, Four Crosses, Coed-y-Dinas and Glanmule (Gibson, 2002).

Welsh henge monuments appear to be influenced by eastern contact. Lynch believes their construction may have caused some resentment, as evidenced at Bryn Celli Ddu (Anglesey) where the henge was subsequently buried beneath an older style tomb (Lynch 1991, 94-5) proving that old traditions were still strong. However, there is evidence that the south and east of Wales embraced the new monuments and ideas more quickly. Most notably, the Hindwell

Bryn Celli Ddu, Anglesey

enclosure in Radnorshire, which dates to 2500 BC, contained 1,530 posts up to 6 metres high.

Stone Circles begin to appear late in the period in the uplands and share several traits with henges. They are both open air and circular in plan and unassociated with primary burials, although cremations may be added later. They are normally found within a group of other monuments (perhaps standing stones, a twin circle, cairns) and are located at important nodal points along routes and lines of communication such as cross-ridge paths. This location at territorial peripheries and along tracks suggest use by more than one group. All Montgomeryshire's stone circles, except the possible circle beneath the henge at Dyffryn Lane, Berriew, have been found in the uplands, particularly near ridges. But perhaps these survive as they have been in areas less subjected to subsequent agricultural developments, although it does appear that in Montgomeryshire none of the lower-lying timber henges were replaced with stone. Wales boasts over 80 Stone Circles, most of which appear in groups of two or more, such as those in the Kerry Hills in Montgomeryshire. Some stone circles appear to have astronomical alignment, and being on open hills with wide views of the sky could have been built as calendrical monuments based on celestial movement. Some circles are embellished with a bank of cairn materials and these are often associated with primary and/or secondary burials over a number of years. Evidence at some circles across Wales suggests a variety of ceremonies performed within the circle involving the burial of charcoal, which may be significant of a pyre. Ring cairns are frequently found in complexes or within cemeteries (Lynch *et al*).

Ring ditches appear at the end of this period, usually occurring in groups and in proximity to other monuments, and are often all that is left of a burial monument, no doubt the ditch created by the soil required to cover the burial. Depositions including pottery are frequently associated with ring ditches. The ditch at Tyr Gwyn Mawr, Elmtree Farm, Montgomeryshire probably dates from the Beaker period at the transition from the third to second millennium BC (Gibson, 1992). Four other ditches are in close proximity, all located on a terrace sloping down to the Severn/Vyrnwy floodplain.

Single standing stones begin to appear during the Late Neolithic and proliferate during the early Bronze Age. It is extremely difficult to ascertain the distribution of these monuments because of their ease of removal and destruction. In the uplands, standing stones are often located on trackways and may be interpreted as border or directional markers or public memorials. Other standing stones are found in complexes and in association with stone circles. These are generally tall and may constitute markers because of their visibility at a distance. Many of these complexes also include stone avenues and alignments, sometimes of very small stones. In Montgomeryshire, the stone avenues at Carreg Llwyd, Trannon Moor, Carno and at Lluest Uchaf, Caersws both comprise very small stones and are both associated with standing stones and nearby cairns.

Cairn construction in upland areas increases during the same period, reflecting an expansion of population (Gibson, 1993).

As the Welsh Neolithic comes to a close and the Bronze Age begins, changes in material culture occur alongside conceptual changes, one of which was the perception of time. Time is a central theme in ritual, particularly social time (the history of a group and individual) and ritual time (comparative existence of past, present and future). In ancient times, the past, present and future were contemporaneous, as reflected by communal graves and anonymous ancestral groups remaining an essential part of the community, and the knowledge that in the future when you died you would join this group. By the late Neolithic, the past was no longer contemporaneous with the present. The dead retained their identity and were placed firmly in a closed past in order to become named progenitors. This validated the territorial, wealth or status claims of the descendants. This concept of lineage became a powerful facet of religion, for a ritual is validated by an antiquity that cannot be refuted or questioned. Ritual also employs archaic language and device no longer in everyday use which effectively prohibits challenge or discussion (Bradley, 1998). In this way, rituals maintain social division by making them part of a timeless, natural order (Bradley, 1998). The monuments themselves are constant visible symbols of continuity, communal achievement, memory and ancestral entitlement.

An interest in circular monuments grows considerably during this time and throughout the coming Bronze Age—nearly all types of monuments found in late Neolithic and early Bronze Age are interpretations of the circular archetype. Circles are found in non-structural rings of boulders under mounds, rings of boulders on the surface of mounds, art on the backs of orthostats, carved decorations on or in a mound's structural elements (Barclodiad yr Gawres), stone settings outside monuments, and timber circles, to name but a few. Ceremonies which formerly took place in the fore-courts of open tombs were more frequently being performed in circular open arenas, with open arenas finally eclipsing the use of large monuments completely.

In the Later Neolithic many chambered tombs were sealed rendering their contents inaccessible, and earthen mounds were enclosed by ditches. All of these changes had the effect of increasing the distance between the living and the dead. Both cremation and group inhumation were practiced in Wales throughout the Neolithic, but probably due to the strength of megalithic traditions, individual inhumations were slow to be adopted in Wales, and the practice was short-lived. Cremation finally became the predominant practice across Wales by around 2000 BC, but until then the deceased continued to be considered a member of society, exerting influence over the living and being added to the communal tomb. Gradually this belief changed, as evidenced by the growing practice of individual inhumation and cremation. It then appears that the deceased, rather than continuing to be a member of society, then became an ancestor from whom lineage could be traced. Spatial relationships in the deposition of cremations and the placement of cremations into existing monuments may have represented relationships of descent further elaborating on the placing of these individuals in the past (Thomas).

Upland domestic evidence in Montgomeryshire is rare. A few possible hut circles were found around the small lakes near Carneddau, and a few casual discoveries of mostly polished axes

Iron Age
900-55BC
Bronze Age
2500-900BC
Neolithic
4000-2500BC

Chiefdoms and warrior caste formed during the early Bronze Age solidify into political entities. Proliferation of ring cairns, stone circles, standing stones, stone rows and highland burial mounds. 1000 BC, Wilburton phase of bronze metallurgy first appears in the Marches and the Severn Valley.

Mesolithic
10,000-4000 BC

From 3000 BC, ritual complexes begun at Trelystan, Four Crosses, Sarn-y-Bryn-Caled, Caebetin Hill, Dyffryn Lane, Llandegai.

Nomadic groups in Montgomeryshire.

From 7,000 BC, temporary visits by hunting parties to the Montgomeryhsire uplands.

Upper Palaeolithic
30,000-10,000BC

Time line showing respective lengths of Prehistoric periods, and summary of activities in Montgomeryshire

attest to activity in the uplands to the west of Newtown and the Dovey valley. However, many structures and artefacts were discovered at the upland site of Trelystan, a ritual complex with continued use over a long period of time. Two or three stakehole structures were dated to between 2900 and 2500 BC. The buildings measured around 4 metres by 4.5 metres and had central, stone-lined hearths containing fire-cracked stones and charcoal. These may have been conical domestic structures with rafters where the uprights are joined at the apex. The interior may have been divided into smaller areas for cooking and sleeping. Flint tools and Grooved ware are associated with the structures, which may have been of a temporary, seasonal domestic nature. Dietery evidence survives in the form of wild raspberry, apple and Poa grass remains along with hazelnut shells. Pottery, burnt bone and flintwork were also found on site. Burnt areas surrounded the structures yielded flintwork (including leaf-shaped arrowheads and flakes), and decorated Grooved Ware pottery sherds that bore evidence of fire use. This pottery was made with materials from a quite distant source. It was evident from the distribution of flintwork that various activities were carried out at pre-specified areas at the site, suggesting an organized workplace. Yet habitation at Trelystan may have been transitory due to the scarcity of resources at this elevation, and it may have been a short-term home part of the year for a semi-mobile group. All of the domestic evidence succeeded a multiple burial.

At Breidden sherds of Peterborough Ware were found beneath a Bronze Age rampart. Two fragments of flintwork and a polished axe were found on the site as well. There is evidence of a structure dated to 1900 BC that measured approximately 4 by 3 metres and which contained hearths or pits and has some similarities to those found at Trelystan. Aerial photography has revealed a possible rectangular structure which may be Neolithic in date (Arnold).

Fifty-six flints dating from the Mesolithic through to the Early Bronze Age were found scattered across the area surrounding Mynydd Carreg-y-big, a ridge at 400 metres OD. The fact that some of these flints were brought from a distance, and that some were retouched, indicate their status as a precious commodity. This scatter could indicate temporary hunting camps set up on the ridge, as this location would not have been suitable for long-term settlement (Silvester, Davies, 1992).A timber circle found at Caebatin Hill, Kerry comprised a small oval circle of stakes, covered by a round barrow. The circle was oriented to the cardinal points with larger posts to the east and west and an edge-set stone at the south (Gibson, 2002).

Afon y Dolou

Neolithic chambered cairn
Location: North of the southern end of Lake Vyrnwy
(SO 019 230)
Access: On open hillside moorland criss-crossed by public paths

Take the B4393 along the northern side of Lake Vyrnwy from the dam. Just past the entrance to the Tower Hotel, cross a bridge and immediately turn right up the narrow lane. Follow this round, bearling left at the fork until you reach a farmyard, with the house on the right and the yard itself on the left. Park somewhere just beyond this.

Just before you reach a gate across the road a couple of hundred yards beyond this farm, a footpath leads up through a gate into the woodland on the right. The path keeps to the left-hand edge of the wood, then passes out into the field on the left over a stile. Follow the line of the fence-come-hedge on the right uphill and cross by another stile into the next field. Turn left and pass through the field gate into a further field. The path now follows the slight dip in the field diagonally uphill to the gap in the bank at the top. Through this gap, the path becomes less distinct, but turns right to shadow the line of the dip in the slope. Some fences have to be clambered across, for one of which you can utilise a stone set in the ground as a semi-stile. The cairn is then on the hillside ahead of you.

Afon y Dolou is located on a spur of the highest peak in the area. With the peak rising behind to the north, the structure looks out over distant mountains to the south, west and east and a small valley directly below to the south and west. The surrounding landscape gives one the impression of being on top of a dome at the centre of a large circle of mountains. This is a well preserved chambered cairn located on a natural shelf below the ridge, facing south along the valley toward the Vyrnwy river. The chamber is rectangular and measures 5 by 2.5 metres. Three standing stones on the north-east side are a possible constricted entrance measuring 1.5 by 6 metres. A low, almost circular bank surrounds the chamber measuring 10.6 metres east to west and 8.6 metres north to south. This may be the remains of a cairn or a ring bank. There are no capstones on site and the area is much disturbed by modern activity despite it being somewhat remote (Gibson, 2002).

Sarn-y-bryn-caled

Neolithic Ritual Complex
Location: South-west of Welshpool (SJ 222 052)
Access: By side of main roads and nature reserve

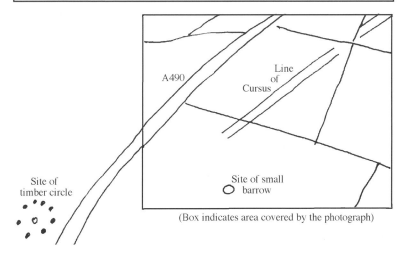

A490

Line
of
Cursus

Site of
timber circle

Site of small
◯ barrow

(Box indicates area covered by the photograph)

From Welshpool take the A490 south for approximately 1.6 miles and park at the car park on the left just before the junction with the A483. The complex is directly off the east side of the highway. The timber circle site is nestled between the A490 and the A483. Coed y Dinas is just on the other side of the pond.

Sarn-y-bryn-caled is one of around 40 timber circles identified so far in Britain, and falls in the middle of the size range at 17 metres in diameter. (The famous Woodhenge is one of the largest at 43 metres in diameter.) Timber circles can be found from central Scotland to south-west England, with one outlying group in Ireland. Sarn-y-bryn-caled is actually a double circle comparable to a similar monument at Oddendale in Cumbria. Together with Dyffryn Lane and Berriew, Sarn-y-bryn-caled forms part of a linear arrange-ment of monuments along the valley floor near Welshpool, possibly relating to the profile of the nearby Breidden mountains.

Major construction took place contemporaneously at all of the complexes around 2000 BC. Earlier construction tends to be labour intensive, grand earthwork sites. Later phases tend toward smaller, more formalized ring ditches and henges—circular cere-monial areas enclosed by a bank and an outer ditch, punctuated by one or more causeways entering the central space. According to Gibson, 'These are less labour intensive but nevertheless retain the sanctity or importance of the area in the religious lives of the population'.

Timber circles predate and in some cases were replaced by stone circles. This close sequential and geographical relationship helps provide some insight as to the appearance of timber circles whose only remaining visible evidence is in the form of post-holes. The original appearance and design of the Sarn-y-bryn-caled monument may be suggested by Stonehenge for example. Scholars have long considered that the mortice and tenon and tongue-and-groove construction at Stonehenge, common woodworking techniques that are unnecessary when dealing with such massive stones, suggest that the builders may have been more accustomed to constructing these structures from timber. Stonehenge may therefore be a stone version of the more familiar wooden monuments exemplified at Sarn-y-bryn-caled, having uprights linked at the top by lintels (Gibson, 1992). Richard Bradley postulates that timber circles, being of a perishable material, having solar alignments and yielding evidence of fasting, may have been associated with the living, while later stone circles erected over them, being non-perishable, having lunar alignments and yielding cremation evidence, may have been associated with the dead and darkness (Bradley, 2005).

The development of Sarn-y-bryn-caled spanned almost 2,000 years, from the late Neolithic to Early Bronze age. This complex, centred around timber circles and a cursus also has two pit circles, two hengiform monuments, a ritual pit and several ring ditches.

The initial monument was a rectangular cursus 10 metres wide by 400 metres long, dating to 3930 BC (Gibson, 1992a). The cursus is aligned north-east to south-west and comprises two parallel ditches with a number of causeways. Modification of the cursus continued until 2695 BC. An isolated posthole from the Neolithic phase suggests the presence of a standing timber post, perhaps revealing a tradition of a wooden counterpart to the later standing stone. Five ring ditches, ranging from 10 to 35 metres in diameter, possibly represent damaged late Neolithic to early Bronze Age barrows.

A horseshoe shaped element, 8 metres in diameter, as suggested by a ditch, was then added. The ditch has rounded terminals 1.2 metres across and 1 metre deep. There is evidence that the ditch may have been accompanied by an outer bank, whilst the ditch itself has been recut indicating continued use. On either side of the causewayed entrance, two posts 40 centimetres in diameter formed an entrance, possibly lintelled. Four cremations were found in the ditch terminals. The primary cremation was accompanied by a flint flake but none of the later burials is associated with grave goods. Sherds of later Neolithic Peterborough Ware as well as a possible wooden object were found in the ditch itself.

An oak timber circle 17.5 metres in diameter comprising 20 posts was added in the early Bronze Age, around 2100 BC. All the posts were large, mainly being around 30 centimetres in diameter, but two were enormous at 70 centimetres in diameter, probably representing an entrance to the circle. The central feature is an inner circle 3 metres in diameter of 6 posts 60-70 centimetres in diameter, and probably taller than the outer circle posts, within which was a large, rectangular pit. There is evidence that this central feature was burned down at some point. East of the central circle are the remains of a two-posted structure, the size of the posts and their placement indicates they may have formed an altar-like structure. A solar alignment is also suggested by the eastern orientation marked by this two-posted structure, as well as the southern orientation established by the two entrance posts in the outer circle. These circles are echoed by concentric stake circles from the same era at both Trelystan and Four Crosses. The central pit, shaped like an inverted pyramid, contained two cremation burials. One of the cremations was originally contained in a bag or basket that also contained four prestigious barbed and tanged flint arrowheads. Evidence indicates that the arrows were contained within the body, suggesting a possible human sacrifice. The second, later cremation was also placed in a basket or bag. A small Food Vessel vase with possible food residue on the inner surface was recovered with the cremation. The latest phase of the complex comprises two ring-ditches at nearby Coed-y-Dinas, where Beaker pottery dated to 2000 BC was found (Gibson, 1992).

The Bronze Age

Early Bronze Age

The Early Bronze Age in Britain spans the period 2,300 BC to 1,500 BC. The climate remained much the same as during the Late Neolithic except that it was slightly drier. Beech and ash trees increased in the woodlands. Brown bears increased in population, whilst the red squirrel made its debut and the auroch became extinct. Pollen analysis reveals that cereal, particularly barley (found at Four Crosses in addition to oats), and other cultivars became more common, though these may have been brought in from other areas. No permanent farmsteads have been found in the Welsh uplands where the pollen was found, and there is still scant evidence for farmsteads in the lowlands. At Stackpole in Pembrokeshire, for example, there are possible plough-marks of Early Bronze Age date within small, embanked fields. Whilst burnt grain has been found at several sites, these may be ritual locations rather than farms and there is little bone evidence of domesticated animals because of acidic soils, although some have been found including pig, wildfowl, sheep and cattle. Upland soils were decimated by deforestation and probably over-grazing and by 1000 BC the blanket of peat which formed over this devastated soil effectively prohibited reforestation and grazing in many areas. Woodland clearances remained fairly small-scale in the lowlands and were not found until the Iron Age.

In the rest of the world, culture was changing rapidly. The first Chinese Dynasty, the Hsia Dynasty, ruled between 2205 and 1766 BC. In 2200 BC, Indo-European invaders brought the earliest form of the Greek language to mainland Greece, giving rise to the Mycenaean Civilization. Between 2000 and 1500 BC the Minoan civilization, based in Knossos on the island of Crete, reached its peak. Between 2000 and 1000 BC, Indo-European immigrants were also making their way to Italy via the Alps. They introduced the horse, the wheeled cart, and bronze crafting to the Italian peninsula laying the seeds of the Roman Empire.

In Britain, settlements are thought to have become semi-permanent, although there continues to be a frustrating scarcity of evidence. Livestock paddocks are evidenced at several sites throughout the country indicating at least some ties to a specific location. Seasonal settlements in the uplands are represented by Cafn Caer Euni in Gwynedd and Trelystan in Montgomeryshire.

Across Britain round stone structures approximately 5 metres in diameter started to occur in both upland and lowland situations (where they are often buried beneath consequent building). These huts are clustered in groups of between four and 28, each group being surrounded by an irregular stone-walled enclosure. However, the land surrounding these settlements is often presently unsuitable for planting, making the economy impossible to determine. Din Lligwy on Anglesey is an example of one of these 'villages'.

Above and opposite: reamains of round stone huts at Din Lligwy, Anglesey

Distribution of these sites may be more widespread than is presently known especially as some may have been constructed of the more perishable wood, but they seem to be rare in southern Wales. Many of the sites that are known have layers of construction indicating continual habitation or re-visitation. Isolated structures such as monuments and possible huts are difficult to date as there is a lack of context.

Kidney-shaped mounds of burnt stone between 10 and 20 metres in diameter have been found deposited near or in watery areas all over Wales, except in the east. They are often found in clusters of four or five and their distribution is echoed by finds of Middle Bronze Age spears and arrowheads indicating hunting associations. Many of these mounds contain pits with evidence of continual use. These may have been used for cooking or are clearance cairns, readying the land for grazing. They were not associated with any domestic sites.

Around 2500, settlement patterns seemed to change. Megalithic tombs were sealed and abandoned and the switch to large, open-air, community-centred monuments with more overt ranking structures was implemented. There appeared to be some social upheaval accompanied by violence throughout Britain. Darvill cites three phases of social change: the blocking of tombs; the abandonment of camps and enclosures coinciding with regeneration of woodland and scrub-grassland in previously cleared areas; and the development of defended camps and warfare. At Crickley Hill, Gloucestershire, hundreds of arrowheads were found providing evidence that the settlement within the defensive rampart was sacked and burnt. At Hambledon Hill, Dorset, several bodies, at least one with an arrowhead in the corpse, were found sprawled in a ditch with part of the defensive embankment collapsed over them. Regeneration of wood and scrub-grassland may have occurred after planting ceased to be viable and the land was abandoned. Population during this time increased and the pressure was greater.

Politics became much more structured during the Early Bronze Age than ever before. The displays of power seen at large communal monuments indicates a stratified society with a focus on the individual, perhaps a chief, rather than on the community. Personal wealth would have been accumulated by such a leader who then controlled the redistribution of goods and services probably through ritual of some kind, such as feasts and public gatherings. This practice remains alive among many tribal societies today. Skills were still probably pooled for communal projects such as monument building, but in exchange for their work, the community would expect protection from starvation, the elements and from other communities who may have been seeking to take control of their resources. This political structure is a natural progression from that of the Mesolithic with its increasingly bounded territories and growing population, itself caused by competition for resources that were once abundant and freely available to all.

Prestige and power became an important survival skill both for the leaders and for the individual communities (Darvill). Individuals began to display their power through visible signs of wealth, and these needed protecting. For example, at Mount Pleasant, Dorset, a palisade of huge tree trunks set ten feet into the ground was built in 1687 +/-63 BC around an area of 11 acres within an earlier henge enclosure. No wonder it has been termed a 'super henge'. New prestige goods were constantly in demand and fashion became big, especially if imported from other areas. Reproductions in cheaper materials soon followed, debasing the

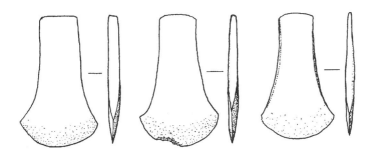

Copper axes found in an early Bronze Age hoard in Flintshire

original prestige item. Bronze daggers were replicated in flint or bone, and bronze axes copied in stone or flint (flintworking enjoyed a resurgence probably due to this market). Prestige items often took the form of personal ornaments in an ostentatious show of power, rank or status. Gold, bronze and copper were the preferred metals for these, embellished with Mediterranean feiance beads, Baltic amber and Jet. New objects had the most value and power, while older objects that may have once had significance became domestic items. Beaker vessels, once strictly grave items, became acceptable as domestic items, while the newer food vessels became the preferred grave item. Collared urns and containers followed. Prestige items are mostly known from burials and depositions, but grave goods also included domestic items such as leaf-shaped arrowheads, transverse arrowheads suitable for bird-hunting, scrapers, bone-points, antler tines, stone or flint axes, polished edge knives, serrated blades, stone rubbers and boar's tusk blades as well as personal ornamentation such as shale beads, bone and metal ornaments and the new Jet belt sliders (invented around 2500 BC, these were intricately carved attachments to leather or fabric belts and in addition to being status items, functioned as adjustable closures). New objects also appear, some of which appear to fit into the category of a prestige item as being of no utilitarian value, including antler maceheads, unwieldy stone and flint axes from far distant sources, and bone skewer-pins (some with elaborated heads). Large Scandinavian axes are sometimes found in hoards in southern England, whilst Irish flat copper axes appear in Wales and elsewhere in England. Curious humans love exotic items.

Rules governing the acquisition, use and disposal of these objects were probably fairly stringent. Richard Bradley contends that there were several structured spheres of exchange operating at different levels of society. The general community would have access to local networks dealing with domestic items such as pottery and quernstones as well as raw materials such as flint and stone. Another echelon of the community, perhaps chiefs or religious leaders, may have had access to long-distance alliances exchanging the most valuable goods and knowledge. This economic situation would have maintained the value of these goods by making them difficult for the common folk to obtain. Lynch postulates that these items may have been the property of the entire community and were simply curated by the group leaders. Acquisition and deposition of goods reinforced prestige of an individual in life and death. Deposition began to take on greater significance and increased in popularity during this time. Hoards, primarily of metal weaponry, are found in many natural settings, especially near water, unassociated with monuments.

Bronze Age peoples had extensive communication networks facilitated by interconnecting trackways linking communities within a region as well as connecting to long-distance routes for exchange and trade. Such trackways often sprouted monuments. In Montgomeryshire, for example, monuments along the Kerry Ridgeway identified the first major route to and from the Severn and Wye valleys. Boats were another means of communication and trade. The boats of Caldicot Castle Lake date to between 1874 and 1689 BC and are the oldest found specimens in Britain, although recent dating of the boats discovered at Ferriby (Humberside) may push the horizon back even earlier to 2000 BC (Gifford). These latter long and narrow boats were constructed of oak planks sealed with yew stitching and moss caulking. Equipped with square sails and paddles, they were capable of fairly long-distance travel (Gifford). Another style of boat, the coracle, a round, flat-bottomed boat constructed of a wooden frame covered in hide, still survives today. Boats were also trading in the Bristol Channel, the Severn Estuary and elsewhere along the coast.

The complex assemblage of grave and domestic goods from this period indicates a myriad of thriving industries including stone, flint, metal, bone and antler-working, ceramics, and perhaps textile-making. The use of buttons suggests leather clothing, whilst the appearance of pins around 2000 BC indicates the manufacture of woven cloaks and tunics similar to modern kilts (Lynch). Innovations in the stone industry included mace-heads, battle-axes, axe-hammers and shaft-hole adzes. The most elegant of these became grave goods. The personal ornament trade was booming, as was the production of splendid weaponry and accompanying gear such as shields and helmets, perhaps also involving leatherwork. Art and decoration became more ornate, appearing on many products of the day. Trade and foreign relationships, particularly with northern Europe and Ireland were vital to Bronze Age industry. Ireland not only provided the inspiration and prototypes for metal goods, but also for passage graves such as was seen at Barclodiad y Gawres (Anglesey). Northern Europe provided the Scandinavian flint axes and amber. After around 2000 BC, the focus of trade and communication was directed mostly to the English Channel coastlands. Pottery and metalwork were identical in Britain and northern France and Europe, with those on each side of the Channel benefiting from the other's innovations and resources. Welsh raw materials and products were exported, including copper and gold from prolific mines. European styles were borrowed in the production of Welsh jewelry and weaponry as craftsmen busily replicated fashionable items. Flintworking enjoyed a resurgence.

Around 2400 BC, copper technology began to appear in British burial traditions. The inhumations were of single individuals with grave goods that included red beakers, copper daggers, jet buttons, and stone wristguards. The raw material for the pottery probably originated in the Rhineland, evidencing its deliberate selection over available local materials, perhaps for its colour and/or texture. These beakers may have been intended to look like copper (Burnham). Such burials are, however, rare in Wales.

The first evidence for Welsh metal workshops comes from north-west Wales in the form of simple, one piece stone moulds used for casting dagger blades, axes and other copper or bronze (copper and tin or lead alloy) items. This stage began around 2200 BC. Sheet metalworking came a bit later and was used to produce jewelry, beads, plates and many other bronze and gold objects. The fabulous Mold Cape was produced using this technique. This short shoulder cape is made of sheet gold embellished with amber beads and was found around the shoulders of a young male entombed in a round barrow in Mold. The gold has embossed decoration and is designed to resemble fabric. A leather lining was once attached. The cape would have restricted the movements of the young man in life, so it must have been ceremonial, although many sheet-gold pieces were possibly purely for deposition, like the gold lunula retrieved from a peat bog at Bryncir, Caernarfonshire (Lynch *et al*). Subsequently two-piece moulds used for bronze daggers and spearheads were developed around 1600 BC.

Several mines supplied the necessary materials. Copper and lead came from Halkyn Mountain (Flintshire). Copper was also derived from Parys Mountain on Anglesey, Copa Hill near Aberystwyth, and the enormous operation at Great Orme, Llandudno. The chambers are extremely small at Great Orme leading some to postulate that child labour was used (Lynch *et al*). The mine itself is one of the largest prehistoric mines in the world, comprising a complex network of tunnels, shafts and chambers, and yielding a huge collection of mining tools. All three mines were in business for hundreds of years and reached their peak during the Bronze Age.

Design and metallurgy improved significantly towards the end of the period, culminating in the Acton Park style characterized by a large hoard of objects found at Wrexham. Lead was added to the tin bronze for the first time, improving the metal's versatility. Products associated with this stage were exported to all parts of southern Britain and along the European coast to Germany and Brittany as well as to Ireland, the student having become the master (Lynch *et al*).

Pottery fashions fluctuated during this period, the preponderance of evidence again coming from burial contexts. Cremation became standard and utilized pottery in various ways. Initially the cremated bones were placed in a bag and accompanied by an accessory vessel perhaps holding food or beverages. This is similar to the grave goods accompanying the unburnt bone inhumations of the recent past. But then the practice developed of placing burnt bones in a large pottery vessel, sometimes accompanied by a small (pygmy) cup or accessory vessel. Later, this small cup was placed

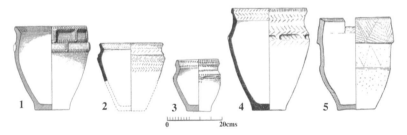

1 Food vessel from Flintshire; 2 Food vessel or urn from Anglesey; 3 & 4 Urn or food vessels from Holt near Wrexham and Anglesey; 5 Collared urn from Denbighshire

inside the cremation vessel, covering the burnt bones. Occasionally, the small cup is the only accompanying vessel. The most common pottery in this context are food vessels and collared urns, the latter originally a domestic item that gradually became more popular for cremations until it became the dominant style. Pottery appears to have become more strictly regional during this time, with no evidence of extensive influences and little trade.

After the sealing and disuse of large chambered tombs, round barrows became the norm, usually clustered in cemeteries around older long barrows and henges, as at Stonehenge and Four Crosses. At the same time funereal ritual seems to have become more complex. One possible scenario is described by James Dyer as follows: the body may have lain in state for quite some time, suffering some decay. The corpse was then burned on a funeral pyre, the bones washed clean of any ashes, placed in urns, bags or boxes and transported to the burial site for deposition. A feast or ceremony would have been held near the burial site, after which the bones would be placed in a pit at the centre of the site, over which a temporary wooden structure was erected. A few days later a barrow mound would be constructed from turves dug from an encircling ditch. Finally, a lintelled timber circle might be erected around the barrow (Dyer, 2002, 70-71). This is just one possible interpretation of available evidence. Elaborate processes such as this are evidenced at several sites, but the exact nature of the proceedings cannot truly be known. There is certainly evidence that funeral pyres were sometimes used and a variety of log coffins, leather or textile bags, pottery vessels and hollowed tree trunks were used as receptacles for the burnt bone. Bones were sometimes washed prior to placement in the receptacle, sometimes charcoal from the pyre is present. The burial itself may be in a hole, in a stone cist or on the ground surface. In some cases, the container is protected from breakage by being placed in a larger urn. Several North Welsh burials yielded infant earbones, 'hinting at less comforting funerary rites' (Lynch *et al*).

Burials of the rich were usually covered with newly constructed individual barrows. In general, however, multiple graves were covered in one barrow in a final act. Grave goods including personal ornaments, metalwork, pottery or tools usually accompanied inhumations. Causewayed enclosures were abandoned for the most part, but some were revisited and modified. Long barrows, bank barrows and, in Wales, primarily round barrows, some with passage graves, appeared more frequently, replacing chambered tombs and long mounds. (A few long mounds/barrows evidencing later activity have been discovered in southern England and Wales, but these are rare and may represent a temporary return to older traditions.)

The use and construction of henges and cursus increased after 2500 BC, but began to decline after the turn of the millennium and were out of use by around 1900 BC. Instead stone circles, standing stones, stone rows and avenues, barrows and cairns became the main monuments. Stone circles themselves also became much bigger in diameter around 1700 BC, and the stones more widely spaced. Stones replaced the timber circles at Woodhenge and Stonehenge.

The complexes at Four Crosses and Trelystan continued to be modified during this time through the early second millennium when the use of a single mound as a cemetery became the standard practice in Wales. These cemeteries were fairly long-lived, some continuing in use until 1000 BC. Many earthen barrows and cairns are located near trackways, on ridges and promontories and may have served as territorial and directional markers (Lynch). The proliferation of smaller mounds in the uplands indicates increased settlement and exploitation with some cairns simply reflecting ground clearance; there is barely a ridge in Montgomeryshire where one does not find a small cairn or mound. Weaponry is rare in

Welsh Early Bronze Age graves, corresponding with the preference for a fairly communal cemetery mound. 'The warrior does not appear as the admired ideal and it is fitting that the most spectacular symbol of power from Wales, the gold cape from Mold, was a priestly garment which could not have been worn by a fighting man' (Lynch, 138).

In the Early Bronze Age, the population expanded into the uplands of Montgomeryshire as evidenced by collared urn burials and artefact finds. Pastoralism was evidently the dominant economy in the uplands, for pollen data indicates continued forest clearance from the Neolithic period onwards. This may also have meant that any houses were built of wood, as evidenced at Trelystan, and so have left little trace. Yet upland cairnfields represent a long-term investment in the land by people who made improvements and built permanent ritual structures—sites that have been initially interpreted as domestic often turn out to be ritual or funereal upon further excavation. Therefore it is likely that the uplands were settled or at least managed continually until the Iron Age. The Cambrian Mountains present a typical Bronze Age upland landscape including cairns, ceremonial monuments, and possible huts. Nearby, on Bugeilyn Moor, Bronze Age arrowheads were found, possibly representing ceremonial depositions (Arnold).

Valleys continued to be exploited during this time as well, as seen in other areas of Wales. Data from the Breidden pond suggests clearance of the area around 2000 BC with some regeneration following, and a new phase of clearing around 1500 BC. Clearances at the upland area of Carneddau began in the early Bronze Age and ended at the end of the period, between 1600 and 1200 BC (Gibson 1993). Palaeoenvironmentalists examined pollen preserved in local peat deposits and carbonised plant remains recovered during excavation of two cairns at Carneddau and have determined that woodland clearance and expansion of open grassland, possibly for grazing, was already well under way by the time the cairns were built. There is also some evidence for cultivation. Dates obtained from burials start at 2000 BC and continue until 1500 BC (Gibson, 1989).

New ideas appeared earlier in Montgomeryshire than in much of the rest of Wales, probably due to trade and exchange between the

Severn Valley and southern England. Severn Valley burials of early Bronze Age date began to include daggers, and depositions or hoards of metal weapons began to become common. This region appears to share more cultural aspects with the chiefdoms of Wessex than with other parts of Wales (Lynch).

Beaker pottery went out of use in funereal contexts when inhumation was replaced by cremation. There is only one definite example of a Beaker burial in Montgomeryshire, that of a single inhumation in a grave at Darowen near Machynlleth, a burial accompanied by Irish bronze knives. A second Beaker was found nearby beneath a large stone during road construction, and is probably from another burial. Beaker sherds were also discovered in buried soils and mound material at Trelystan, dated between 2300–1710 BC.

Early Bronze Age implements are rare. Darowen and Four Crosses yielded a few daggers dated between 2200–2000 BC, and a flat axe was recovered at Carno dated to 1700 BC. A one-sided sandstone mold for casting flat triangular daggers and possibly axes was found in Newtown. This was one of the earliest recovered manufacturing artefacts from the Welsh metallurgical industry. Four Crosses yielded a V-perforated jet button. At Breidden, star-shaped faience beads dated from 2100–1700 were found, whilst a fine flint dagger was included in a grave near Trefeglwys. 'It is possible that objects were placed in graves at times of stress in society, when it was felt necessary to make a statement about a

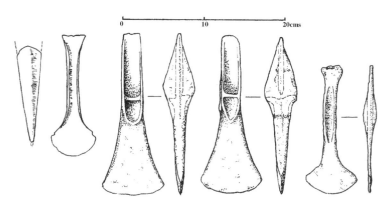

Early palstave hoard from Denbighshire

70

person's status, as perhaps with the Darowen and Four Crosses burials. This practice declined through the Bronze Age' (Arnold).

Concentrations of burials and other monuments are found on the Kerry hills, particularly near Vyrnwy, Esgair Cwmowen, Mochdre and Llangadfan. The sheer number of burial monuments found in upland locations may be interpreted in different ways. There may have been greater population pressures between 2000 and 1500 BC leading to the exploitation of lands previously considered marginal. So little Neolithic evidence remains, however, that this hypothesis may be rash. What Neolithic evidence that may remain is probably hidden beneath later sites and will only be discovered during future excavations. Alternatively, one can argue that there may have been little or no increase in population, as artefact distribution is similar in the Bronze Age as to the Neolithic, suggesting that population remained fairly constant. Perhaps upland locations appear to be more numerous than lowland locations because of a higher survival rate of monuments in upland areas. Settlement may have been restricted to lowlands and the uplands used exclusively for grazing and hunting. This may be indicated by pollen from the upland side of Carneddau indicating grasslands, while the lowland sites of Breidden and Coed-y-Dinas indicate cereals.

Following the pattern established in the rest of Britain, henges appeared to decline in use by around 1900 BC, while round cairns and mounds increased dramatically. Ring ditches began to appear around 1800 BC in clusters or cemeteries, but some or all of these may represent the remains of ploughed out round barrows. As with other monument types, the concentration of groupings in fertile areas probably reflects the greater availability of labour. Many ring ditches have been identified in the upper Severn Valley, ranging between 5 and 30 metres in diameter except for the larger Carreghofa and Sarn-y-bryn-caled (both between 40 and 60 metres in diameter). The bulk of Montgomeryshire ring ditches are between 10 and 20 metres in diameter (70 examples) with 54 large examples between 20 and 30 metres in diameter and 20 small examples between 5 and 10 metres in diameter. Smaller monuments are found clustered around larger ones. Twr Gwyn Mawr, Moel Tryfel and Cefn Llwyd are such sites in Montgomeryshire. At Dyffryn Lane, Berriew, a cemetery of 10 ring ditches surrounds a central henge and larger barrow. Burials have been found at a small ring ditch at Four Crosses, Berriew with a possible late Neolithic date. Cremations have been recovered from ditches, but never a central burial, suggesting that the ditches became used as cemeteries (Gibson, 2002).

Round barrows proliferated over Montgomeryshire beginning in the early Bronze Age. These barrows cover inhumation or cremation burials, but were used for only a fraction of society. Round barrows may be entirely or partially earthen (barrows) or stone (cairns). Cairns may be further defined by ring banks (ring cairns) or stone kerbs (kerb cairns). Some cairns may have evidence of timber structures or palisades. There are at least 315 round barrows widely distributed across the upper Severn Valley including 142 cairns, 12 ring cairns, and 29 structured cairns. Most cairns are smaller than 20 metres in diameter, but a few can be between 20 and 30 metres in diameter. Barrows under 10 metres in diameter are found more often in the western areas of the region, while medium sized examples lie in the uplands and river valleys. The largest barrows, over 30 metres in diameter are found almost exclusively in the Severn Valley. This is the most fertile location in the region, and may have been home to a greater population with a greater availability of labour. Placement of barrows undoubtedly had some significance, concentrating on access routes and dramatic landscape features. Tyr Gwyn, dominating the Trannon Moor sites, was constructed midway between two major valleys and on the only cross-moor paths in the area, formalizing an ancient route. Many are located near water and emphasize watersheds and other important watery places. A concentration of barrows and ring ditches is located at the mouths of the Tanat, Cain and Vyrnwy rivers, marking the point where the Severn flows out of the Welsh valleys and into the Midlands plain. As has been suggested before, this was probably an important access point into and out of the uplands. Some patterning can be discerned in upland barrow distribution. Cairns located on mountaintops, crests or ridges tend to dominate their horizon, as at Carnedd Das Eithin. Their dominance over the landscape highlights their significance. In Kerry, Caebetin is located on a hilltop on the watershed between the Mule and Nant Miheli. This cairn is intervisible with Kerry Two Tumps and Glog

Hill, creating a ritual skyline. At Pen-y-bon-fawr, Carnedd Cerrig is an imposing 3 metres tall and dominates the horizon from its mountaintop location. Some sites were probably chosen for the views from their locations—ancestral homelands like the Breiddens were visible from many hilltop, crest and ridge-sited cairns. However, some cairns, even those located on hilltops are invisible until you are close.

Upon excavation of some of these burials, older burials are discovered underneath. The older deposits occasionally yield pottery, from which radiocarbon dates attest late Neolithic / early Bronze Age construction suggesting an early colonization of the uplands. At Carno, two cairns known as Carneddau I and II associated with collared urns, one food vessel and an accessory vessel were found to be dated to between 2500 and 1200 BC. These cairns are intervisible with the Breiddens (Gibson, 1989). Soil analysis suggesting defleshing of bodies prior to cremation indicates that in their earliest phases the cairns were regularly used for sepulchro-ritual activity. A nearby hearth yielded the burnt remnants of an archer's stone wristguard of early Bronze Age style. This hearth was reused many times over the life of the monument. Directly prior to the cairn's construction, charcoal was taken from the hearth and laid in a circle around the central area upon which basal stones were laid. The charcoal may have been used to seal the cremation pits for four cists that were located in the stone ring. The easternmost was empty. The western cist contained a cremation accompanied by a flint knife and flake. The southeastern cist contained a food vessel sherd and remnants of a cremation, the only time a food vessel is found later than a collared urn in a cairn or barrow. The fourth cist contained what was probably the earliest burial, and included an inverted collared urn cremation, the vessel being one of the largest collared urns found so far in Wales. A satellite cairn was added to the main cairn at its northern arc and covered a cremation pit containing over a kilo of cremated bone. Pyro-ritual activity was evident in the north-western and north-eastern arcs of the circle, aligning with the maximum rising and setting points of the midsummer sun. This northern arc echoes the cardinal point orientation of many stone circles (Gibson, 1989).

Montgomeryshire boasts 12 stone circles of varying styles. Several are true circles, as at Llyn-y-Tarw, Aberhafesp, while others, such as the Druid Circle on the Kerry Hills are flattened circles, some with a central stone. Many of the circles are constructed of large numbers of small stones whereas some, such as Lled Croen Yr Ych (Llanbrynmair, Montgomeryshire) have small numbers of large stones. Most circles in the Severn Valley region are smaller than the British average and are also comprised of smaller stones making them later in the sequence according to Burl (Gibson 2002). Some archaeologists believe that the earlier larger sites were located farther away from settlements, while later sites appear on the periphery overlooking settlements. Rhos-y-Beddau and Cwm Rhiwiau, both at Llanrhaeadr-ym-Mochnant, Y Capel at Dwyriw and Llyn-y-Tarw II at Caersws were probably peripheral to settlements, given the proximity of associated cairn-fields.

Some of the stone circles have outlying stones and/or accompanying stone rows. There are two stone circles at Llanrheadr-ym-Mochnant. The first, Rhos-y-Beddau, is comprised of 12 stones with a gap in the north-west arc. The stones are low, all under 0.6 metres high and the circle is associated with stone rows running up to but not abutting it. A small cairn is also associated with the monuments. A large quartz boulder may be a marker. There is ancient precedence for the importance of quartz, however, and this crystalline stone may have ritual significance. The second, Cwm Rhiwiau, lies on a plateau 400 metres north of Rhos-y-Beddau. This is an egg-shaped 'circle' measuring 11.4 by 10.5 metres. The stones measure between 0.12 and 0.4 metres in height, with an outlying stone 3 metres to the north and another 20 metres to the south. The monument is roughly aligned with Rhos-y-Beddau.

Some stone circles are thought to be associated with stone axe factories because of their proximity. In Montgomeryshire, at least three circles lie close to the factory at Cwm Mawr, Hyssington, as well as two in Shropshire: Mitchell's Fold and Black Marsh.

A stone circle known as the Kerry Hill Circle, or locally as the Druid Stones, lies on the Kerry Ridgeway. This circle, 26.5 metres in diameter, comprises eight stones 10 metres apart with a large, flat central stone. The outer stones are set tangentially to the central stone. Traces of a bank remain at the northern arc, but this may be the result of grazing damage.

The Llyn-y-Tarw complex in Caersws contains two stone circles. Llyn-y-Tarw I, 19 metres in diameter, comprises 39 stones on a level terrace of a south-east facing slope. Llyn-y-Tarw II also lies on a small plateau, is 13 metres in diameter, and comprises ten small, low stones. The possible remains of a cairn was found in the centre. The area surrounding these circles contains many edge-set stones, cairns and other possible monuments.

Standing stones appear in both uplands and lowlands. Like stone circles, the tradition of standing stones may have been preceeded by or have had contemporary wooden counterparts as suggested by an isolated Neolithic posthole at Sarn-y-bryn-caled. They are not easy to date, but are assumed to be Bronze Age with some Neolithic origins (Gibson 2002). 129 stone circles have been located in Montgomeryshire, made of local, unworked rock. Many are damaged. Montgomeryshire's standing stones tend to be fairly small compared to other stones in Wales and across Britain, Maesmochnant being the tallest at 3.6 metres. They can be found on trackways, ridges and at other highly visible locations suggesting that some are territorial and directional markers, for example Esair-y-groes and Carreg Slican, both at Trefeglwys. Many are found near water, where they may serve as both direc-tional markers and ritual monuments. For example, Carreg Llwyd, Aberhafesp and Ystrad Fawr, Llanbrynmair both lie at the heads of bogs; Eunant Fach, Ffridd Fach Llanwddyn and Graig Wen, Llangynog lie near streams; Maen Bueno and Forden Gaer lie on either side of a fording point of the Severn at Berriew; Maesmochnant at Llanrhaeadr-ym-Mochnant stands close to the Tanat river. Moel y Tryfel, Banwy is located near a stream and beside a track over the Mynydd Dyfnant, suggesting its use as a route marker. Some standing stones are outliers to stone circles, as at Rhos-y-Beddau, aligning the monument to celestial bodies or cardinal points. Many standing stones are associated with one or more monuments, for example Carreg Hir at Caersws stands on a bridleway between Llyn Mawr and Llyn Du. The bridleway continues up towards Llyn-y-Tarw and the ridgeway along Mynydd Clogau on which some large cairns were found. Llyn Mawr Cairn

II is intervisible from this stone, lying on the same track and having its own standing stone built into the monument. Upland sites frequently refer (in orientation of the longer face vis a vis the shorter face, alignment and intervisibility) to the associated valley and the Breidden and Corndon hills. These therefore may be geographical reference points for ancestral origins, or have a purely functional role. As Gibson says: 'If the upland economy is a pastoralist one, then the main Severn Valley landmarks may also have served as referencing points for local granaries and markets for surplus produce' (Gibson, 2002).

Rows are less common but there are at least 5 and possibly 7 examples. All are associated with nearby burial mounds, standing stones and/or circles. It is thought that longer monuments were earlier, dated to 2200–1600 BC, while short rows date from 1800–1200 BC (Gibson 2002). According to this theory, Severn Valley rows date between 2200 through 1200 BC, with Rhos-y-Beddau falling at the early end of the sequence, with the loosely defined rows of Carreg Wen and Faullt later. Rhos-y-Beddau at Llanrhaedr-ym-Mochnant is the best known stone row in the area, running 60 metres eastwards, stopping 8 metres short of the Rhos-y-Beddau stone circle. The row runs along the valley floor, pointing to its head and the two lines of stones converge

Cerrig yr Helfa stone row, Montgomeryshire

76

Carreg Llwyd stone row, Trannon Moor, Montgomeryshire

(from 4 metres apart to 2 metres apart) as they approach the circle. Two phases of construction are suggested by the fact that the easternmost 12 metres of the row has a slightly different alignment and does not widen. Twelve stones remain in the northern row and are smaller than those in the southern row with its 24 remaining stones. Another row is seen at Tryfel. This row runs north to south on a spur above the Afon Twrch valley and comprises eight pairs of stones 1 metre apart. The largest stone is 0.3 metres high, and so this row is difficult to see in the landscape. At its uphill, northernmost end the row terminates in a kerbed cairn. On the Trannon moor at Carno, a single stone row known as Carreg Llwyd can be found. The row runs 21 metres northwards from a large recumbent stone and comprises six to seven large stones. This row is associated with two nearby cairns and several standing stones. Lluest Uchaf at Caersws is located near to the Llyn-y-Tarw monuments. It comprises a single row of 11 stones running 12 metres north to south on the southern, down-ward-sloping terminal end of a ridge which marks the highest point in the immediate landscape, overlooking the ritual landscape below.

The tallest stone is 0.5 metres high. The longer axis of all except the central stone are aligned with the row, with the southernmost stone being just slightly off alignment. The central stone's longer side is perpendicular to the row's alignment, and has large stones piled around the base. Cerrig yr Helfa, Mynydd Dyfnant comprises ten stones, although some may be missing as there are unusual gaps in the construction. A pit or cist may have been central to the monument, making this row sepulchral like others in the area.

Two stone pairs have been discovered in Montgomeryshire dating to the Middle Bronze Age. The first and better known of the two is Carreg Wen in Llanidloes, also known as Y Fuwch Wen a'r Llo (white cow and calf). The stones once stood 2 and 1.25 metres high next to one another on a moor near the source of the Severn, but only the larger stone is visible today (Gibson, 2002). The second pair is Fuallt in Llandinam. These stones are 10 metres apart, aligned north-east towards the Breidden Hills and south-west towards a large cairn on the horizon (Gibson 2002).

Ritual complexes continued to appear during this time. The upland site of Carneddau, Carno, Montgomeryshire spans from 2000 to 1500 BC, the early Bronze Age, and is roughly contemporary with larger complexes in Montgomeryshire. Two ring cairns with associated cremation burials were discovered along with collared urn vessels.

Modifications to existing complexes continued at Four Crosses, Sarn-y-bryn-caled and Trelystan revealing classic Bronze Age sequences. The earliest phases of Bronze Age burials at all of the sites are cremations stored in organic containers and deposited in mound-covered pits, major construction taking place contemporaneously at all of the complexes around 2000 BC. At Four Crosses, food vessel cremations were deposited in separate mounds between 2100 and 1900 BC. At Trelystan, three food vessel cremations were added before 1800 BC. Pit circles appear at Sarn-y-bryn-caled as well as at Four Crosses, perhaps echoed by the concentric stake circles found at both Trelystan and Four Crosses. At Trelystan these were constructed around burial mounds during the second construction phase sometime before 1800 BC (Arnold), consolidating them. The stake circles at Four Crosses were erected between 1900–1600 BC around two large barrows. A stake circle was also found surrounding the barrow at Caebetin Hill, Kerry. The stake circles at Trelystan and Four Crosses were connected by wooden timbers, a form of construction comprising both linear and circular elements that reflects the association of cursus to henges and stone rows to stone circles. In all of these cases, the pits/stakes could represent foundations for roofed wooden structures, but there is no evidence to support this idea. The presence of timber posts at the centre in some of the barrows (Trelystan, Four Crosses, Clywedog) may be a variation on standing stones in barrows recorded elsewhere.

The final change during this period is represented at Trelystan, when the practice of placing single cremations in individual barrows and cairns was replaced by the practice of placing many cremations into existing barrows. The cremations were inserted into the sides and top of two barrows, each having its own separate place (as opposed to the ancient practice of mingling the bones of several individuals together). Twelve cremations of almost equal numbers of female and male adults, with one child, were discovered. Cremations, once stored in organic containers, began to be stored in small and then larger ceramic containers.

Nine possible cists (unassociated with a covering mound) are recorded, all in the upper Tanat Valley. However, the former presence of a mound has to be considered, since all of the sites were damaged. Several of these cist burials have been associated with a complex—Nant Llwyn Gwern, Ffordd Gefn and Drum Llethr, all in Llangynog, and Moel Bwlch Sych at Pen y Bont Fawr all lie within areas of cairns and other monuments. A quirky aspect of cist burial of this area and period is the placement of cremations slightly off centre within the cist. This is seen at Clywedog, Caebetin, Staylittle, Four Crosses and Trelystan. Clywedog contained a young adult female accompanied by a bronze awl dated to 1850 BC. A robbing trench connected to the burial mound yielded two cordoned urns and a small accessory vessel of local materials, but of a style rarely found in Wales. Collared urn burials are represented at Lan Fawr in Churchstoke, Caebetin in Kerry and at Staylittle. The burial at Lan Fawr comprised an inverted urn placed over the cremation of a two-year-old child. The burial site was in a rock-cut pit and covered by a cairn dated to 1600 BC. It has been suggested by Richard Bradley that urns may have been overturned to represent roundhouses, classic domestic structures of the time. Similarly round mounds themselves echo roundhouses much as long mounds were thought to echo domestic longhouses of the early Neolithic (Bradley, 1998). A slightly more disturbing practice may be represented at Sarn-y-bryn-caled. At the centre of the timber circle built about 2100 BC is a pit containing a male burial. A number of fine barbed and tanged flint arrowheads were found there and are thought to have entered the pit inside the corpse, suggesting human sacrifice (CPAT).

Conclusion to the Early Bronze Age

Although there is very little evidence of permanent settlement or domestic evidence of any kind, pollen analysis suggests an increase in woodland clearing as well as the presence of domestic cultivars during the Early Bronze Age. These cleared spaces were also used for grazing animals. Competition for limited resources may have encouraged the development of agriculture.

The social impact of farming was enormous, introducing new material culture and a sedentary way of life that itself brought dramatic cultural changes including wealth acquisition and status. As we have seen from monumental evidence and grave goods, the importance of the individual religious or group leader has Palaeolithic roots, but doesn't become a dominant value until the Bronze Age (perhaps this concept is reaching its apex in current society). The richest burials include a wide array of prestige items and grave goods, making a statement about the status of the dead individual and perhaps the privileges and expectations of the successors. Some of the richest burials are located nearest to the central ancestral monument which certainly lends more legitimacy to the claim of the descendants. Burials within sacred monuments may be the most important of all. Richard Bradley postulates three effects of these later inhumations: the burial may be the final act performed at the monument, giving closure to a long period of ritual use; the burial is an appropriation of the past for the commemoration of a few individuals; the burial may be an attempt to harness the sacred properties inherent in the monument, cementing identification with place to particular members of the community at the exclusion of others (Bradley, 1998).

During the Early Bronze Age, it was understood that the initial burial was the first stage of a continuous and lengthy process. Causewayed enclosures, originally primarily associated with clusters of domestic structures began to be built in separate settings. These were the centre of the religious world, with other monuments clustered around them. These monuments were symbolic of the nucleated settlements of the past. They echoed ancient migration routes and movements of the people. As settlement patterns began to diversify during the later Bronze Age, so did burial monuments, appearing individually across the landscape.

Middle Bronze Age

The British Middle Bronze Age spans from 1500 BC through 1100 BC. During this time many cultures throughout the ancient world were in transition. It was during this period that, elsewhere in the world, Moses and the Israelites left Egypt for the 'promised land' (1250 BC), whilst in Greece, the militaristic Mycenaean civilization dominated the Minoan civilization after destroying their capital, Knossos.

In Britain weather conditions deteriorated throughout the period until the onset of the Sub-Atlantic climatic phase with its high winds, heavy rainfall and much lower temperatures between 1250 and 400 BC. This climatic change dramatically influenced settlement patterns and cultural changes (Lynch). During the worst periods, between 1200 and 900 BC and between 800 and 470 BC, coastal regions including the Gwent and Somerset levels were largely abandoned due to rising sea levels. The growing season became too short for upland crops, leading to diminished population in the uplands across Wales. Settlement hinterlands contracted with a smaller area for agriculture and grazing being exploited. Reliance on livestock increased (Burnham). During favourable periods, the climate supported expansion into upland areas and areas with poorer soils (Darvill), leading to a very high density of prehistoric settlements in these areas. This intensification caused the rapid exhaustion of available soils, and in combination with the rainfall this caused widespread peat bog formation (Burnham). Blanket peat bog causes soil infertility, preventing re-afforestation and leading to the formation of upland moors, which still remain today. In the valleys, forest clearances continued through the Iron Age and into the Roman Era, leading to a permanent reduction of woodland and a proliferation of grasslands. The heavy rainfall also caused the formation of many wetlands and marshy areas in the valleys, but people were able to adapt to these landscapes using new strategies and technologies, especially woodworking. Houses, called crannogs, came to be built in many a lake or lagoon, whilst platforms and trackways were constructed using thousands of worked planks and posts.

There were probably communal meeting places across the country where exchange and trade were carried out. Exchange was widespread and included tools as well as prestige items. Bronze became the most sought after metal, even surpassing the lure of gold in this period; fine bronze weaponry was the most important trade item due to its great prestige value. Transportation was facilitated by the introduction of the horse some time around 2000 BC,

Map showing distribution of Bronze Age sites across Montgomeryshire

and gradually horses became more of a necessity than a luxury for warriors, traders, farmers and the general population. From the tenth century BC, horsemanship took on more importance. Finely crafted horse fittings were made of gold, antler and bronze, many similar to continental European equestrian pieces. The wheel was used on the continent from 2000 BC, but the date of its introduction to Britain is uncertain. There were no roads in Britain at this time, making wagon travel difficult especially in the north and west where the terrain is rugged. No horse fittings were found in these areas either (Darvill).

Sharply defined groups existed within bounded territories. Claims to these territories were validated through ancestral ties reflected and emphasized by burial and ceremonial practice. The power of an individual leader was validated by lineage and made visible by the display of prestige items including personal ornaments, horse-fittings and weaponry.

Field systems become more prominent during the Middle Bronze Age, with evidence of square or rectangular units on slopes and in lowlands. These may have been preplanned as a set of fields, or may reflect additions and modifications to a single, original field. The fields were usually enclosed by banks, ditches or hedges. Residences were scattered among the fields, sometimes singly and sometimes clustered within an enclosure. A typical domestic setting is illustrated at Shearplace Hill, Dorset, in a well populated area along the south coast. Shearplace Hill itself comprised two structures, perhaps a house and a byre, dated to 1180 +/- 180 BC. The 'house' was circular, around 7 metres in diameter with two concentric rings of postholes. Textile production was practiced, as evidenced by the discovery of a weaving comb. The two structures, as well as a working area and a pond were all clustered within an enclosure, outside which lay a stock pen and garden area whilst several fields surrounded the settlement, leading to a trackway that joined with other settlements (Darvill). Cattle, sheep and pigs were kept.

A round house, possibly a domestic structure, 9 metres in diameter was discovered in the valley bottom at Glanfeinion near Llandinam (Britnell et al. 1997). Domestic evidence in general is, however, rare for this period. Stackpole Warren on the south coast of Pembrokeshire is one of the rare examples, with structures dating from 1880 to 820 +/- 60 BC. Stackpole is an upland site with evidence of a round house similar to other examples from Britain at this time (Lynch), but still no evidence of farming. Indeed, to date no farms have been discovered anywhere in Wales that date to the first half of the second millennium BC (Lynch *et al*). Wooden houses may have existed, but one would have to be comparatively lucky to strike post hole evidence for these structures.

As metallurgy became the dominant industry, flint and stonework declined in importance and quality. Metals worked included bronze, iron and gold. Smiths may have produced work at a centralized workshop, or may have travelled around to the various communities they served. The work was most likely seasonal, producing enough stock for subsequent distribution. The larger items displayed regional similarities, suggesting bigger operations producing rapiers, large spearheads and swords.

Copper mining continued at Parys Mountain on Anglesey, Copa Hill at Aberystwyth and Great Orme at Llandudno (Lynch *et al*). The Northern Welsh bronze industry began to decline, however, as it used a lower tin content and a different copper, perhaps from mines in Mid-Wales. By the end of the mid Bronze Age, a bronze of French origin dominated Wales. Smiths who once made both tools and weapons began to specialize in one or the other. Prestige items were still imported from Ireland, but early Irish flat-axes were

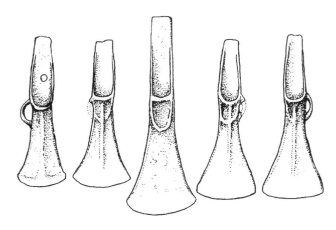

Middle Bronze Age hoard from Cemmaes, Montgomeryshire

replaced by Welsh palstaves, which were more efficient and easier to haft. This style required a more sophisticated double mold (Burnham), and several hoards of experimental palstaves in Wales reflect the continuing innovation of Welsh smiths. Palstaves were an everyday item, a mainstay of working life, much sought after throughout Britain and Europe (Lynch *et al*).

Toward the end of the Middle Bronze Age, weapons increased in number and are more often found in depositional settings. Weapons of British influence are found in northern Welsh hoards, while in the south, weapons of a new continental type begin to appear, for example swords from western France. These weapons reflect changes in fighting and industrial organization that were being introduced into Britain from the continent, and occur simultaneously with economic stress caused by climatic deterioration, suggesting broad political and social unrest (Lynch *et al*). Upheaval was a common theme in the world during that era. In the Mediterranean, raiders known as the Sea People (the Philistines of the Bible) threw the region into chaos, and probably came from or drew mercenaries from northern and central Europe. No-one knows if British individuals joined the party, but the introduction into Britain of Cypriot and Mycenean metalwork of 1300 to 1200 BC style suggests the possibility, although these pieces have been difficult to interpret. European manufacturers gained a great deal of experience in supplying these mercenaries, keeping the British informed of any innovations in weaponry and military technique. The first warrior aristocracy in Europe emerged.

The start of what we think of as Celtic ornamentation began around 1200 BC, with concentrations of gold ornaments including torcs found in large numbers in Ireland and west Wales, as well as Brecon and Radnorshire. These have not been found in graves, and may be purely depositional items (Lynch). Again continental fashions influenced the local style of pins, armlets and torcs, but the metal was close to hand for a South Welsh cluster of Middle Bronze Age gold bracelets and other artefacts indicating that Dolaucothi was a major source of gold at this time (Lynch *et al*).

Domestic industry advanced during the Middle Bronze Age as well. The woodworking industry expanded to include the construction of boats, buildings, trackways and crannog platforms. Whilst widespread, it is poorly represented in the archaeological record due to its survival rate. Seagoing vessels must have existed, but none remain. Plank boats and log boats for river travel have been found dating between 1500 and 750 BC. Textile production became widespread after 1500 BC as evidenced by loom weights, spindle worls and weaving combs found at domestic sites throughout Britain.

Pottery production may have been adversely affected by the economic collapse of the later Middle Bronze Age caused by deterioration in the climate when trade and exchange fell away leaving communities to fend for themselves. Local raw materials were used, no matter the quality, and local potters were in business whatever their skill. Finds in domestic settings are rare and much of what does exist is found to be 'distressingly crude and unimaginative' (Lynch *et al*, p.121).

After 1500 the treatment of the dead began to change. The use of round barrows declined. In Wales, cairns grew smaller, to just 3 to 4 metres across, and were ringed by large kerbstones. These began to appear around 1300 BC when burials were becoming less formalized. Cremation became more prevalent and grave goods less common. Interest in large monuments such as Stonehenge began to diminish. There is evidence that fieldworking began to take precedence over ancient monuments as reflected by the ploughing over of some stone rows and cairns. Some burials were added to earlier monuments, possibly because of a continued reverence for the sacredness of the monument and its ties to ancestors. Use of stake circles increased as seen at Trelystan and Four Crosses noted above, a development also seen in Ireland and continental Europe.

Ritual activity became focused primarily on votive depositions of metalwork, these mainly being made in wet locations, possibly to appease the forces responsible for the rains (Burnham). Between 1600 and 1000 BC, a hoard was deposited at Cemmaes comprising 19 pieces of metalwork including at least seven typical Welsh palstaves. These palstaves have trident patterns on the blades, some having central ribs. A hoard found beneath the peat at Llanerfyl yielded spearheads of leaded bronze with side loops on the socket. A spearhead associated with the barrows at Trelystan provides a rare link between metalwork and burial during the Middle Bronze Age. A dirk with two rivet holes was found at Mynydd Hyddyn completing the full range of Middle Bronze Age weaponry so far found in Montgomeryshire.

Late Bronze Age
The British Late Bronze Age spanned from 1100 to 800 BC, at a time when, in Greece, the cities of Corinth, Athens and Sparta amongst others, thrived along the Aegean coast. Democracy was established in the 5th and 6th centuries BC. In India, the Rig Veda, the first Vedic literature, was written in 1000 BC. Gautama Siddharta Buddha, the founder of Buddhism was born in 563 in Nepal. Rome was founded in 753 and by the 6th century BC had become the dominant power of the surrounding area. In Late Bronze Age central and northern Europe, urnfield cultures, so called for their practice of depositing cremations in ceramic urns in expansive, flat cemeteries, became widespread.

In Britain climatic conditions were fairly dismal until 900 BC and again from 800. Heavy rains, winds and cool temperatures made the uplands challenging and coastal regions uninhabitable until at least 500 BC (Lynch *et al*). During these times the Severn probably experienced extended periods of flooding, causing peat growth in the area, resulting in infertile soil. There is some evidence of settlement with accompanying cultivation and animal husbandry, but most of these settlements were eventually abandoned. Timber track building continued and boatbuilding advanced. But conditions were harsh—based on the average age of remains found in Bronze Age burials in Suffolk, life expectancy for men was around 34, that for women 37.

By this time, almost all groups practised some combination of agriculture and animal husbandry, but long term success depended upon the exploitation of a diversity of landscapes and the production of a surplus. This surplus was required for the sustenance of a growing population and to provide for a group of elite, as well as for exchange. Yet some settlements appear to be 'consumers' rather than 'producers' (Lynch *et al*), and perhaps provided labour or goods to be bartered for the products of farming groups. In Wales, most evidence points to there still being essentially a pastoral economy, though there is some cereal pollen evidence indicating limited agriculture.

Trade was disrupted for a short period following the economic crisis caused by the climatic deterioration of the late Middle Bronze Age. There was a fairly low amount of metal in wide circulation although local workshops flourished. Large-scale and widespread depositional practices may also have been a factor (Lynch *et al*). By the final part of the period, trade and industry began a considerable recovery.

What is known as the Wilburton phase of metallurgy began around 1000 BC, first appearing in Wales in the Marches and the Severn Valley (through evidence from a scrap hoard at Gaer Fawr hillfort). This industry was centred in the south-east of England and used copper imported from central Europe. More lead than had been the case was added to the bronze, allowing for thinner castings, although creating a softer metal. Local smiths under the patronage of a chief or leader manufactured a variety of objects for use by surrounding communities. These smiths were full-time specialists responsible for keeping up with fashions and techniques both invented by their countrymen and those making their way into Britain. Mould designs became more complex, having two and three pieces to create ornate, efficient tools and weaponry. Their products included socketed axes, gouges, narrow-bladed palstaves, socketed sickles, knives, new razors, horse fittings, broad sword blades, tongue chapes (scabbard covers), straight spear ferrules and spearheads (including hollow-bladed and lunate-opening styles). Lunate-opening spearheads are typical spearheads in every respect except that on either side of the lower portion of the blade, near the top of the shaft-fitting, there is a crescent-shaped cut out. A strap may be passed through these cut-outs and tied onto the shaft, strengthening the attachment of the head to the shaft. A hollow-bladed spearhead is simply a spearhead that is not solid metal, but has a hollow tube running almost to the tip into which the pointed shaft fits.This creates a stronger spear due to the combined strength of the tip of the wooden shaft and the metal blade. Gradually these products found their way across Wales.

Further new patterns developed around the 9th century BC with the expansion and formalization of the bronze industry as regional specialists served an increasingly hierarchical society. This became known as the Ewart Park phase. Named after Ewart

Park in Northumberland, this phase began in the 9th century BC, directly following the Wilburton phase. Many aspects of the Wilburton tradition were maintained, with the addition of several innovations. Ewart Park industry is characterised by a larger proportion of lead in the bronze than had previously been used, which allowed a wider range of products to be manufactured. This included horse and wheeled equipment and especially the Ewart Park sword which had two or three holes in the hilt and a longer, more elegant blade than those of previous phases. Beaten bronze sheets were used to make buckets, cauldrons and ceremonial shields, most common in Ireland. There are in fact many regional differences, but some tools and weapons, especially the sword, are common across Britain. Founders' hoards and ritual deposits increased during this time, while the importance of the spear appears to decline.

Tribal networks emerged in areas where local industry was strong such as in south-east Wales where a monopoly emerged as an elite group controlled the manufacture, distribution and mining aspects of the industry over a large area. Smaller regional industries emerged in the north; certainly personal gold ornaments of Irish and local influence were being manufactured in Wales. At the same time a revival of trade began between Ireland, and between eastern England and Europe. Irish gold bracelets and lock-rings, together with European amber beads and harness decorations were found in Anglesey and the northern Welsh coast evidencing trade routes as well as the affluence of these communities (Lynch *et al*). Scrap metal was also traded across long distances, either being deposited in hoards or recycled for use in the metal industry across England and Wales. Mining still continued in parts of north and mid Wales, though it may have been experiencing some difficulty. Mines may have become the property of certain groups as evidenced at Llanymynech Hill, Montgomeryshire, where a copper mine producing zinc-rich ores was protected by a hillfort (see below).

Sheet-metal working became fashionable by the 8th century BC, producing buckets, cauldrons and shields (all prestige items). There was a continuous, insatiable demand for metal goods. Not only were these items highly efficient, but exotic, aesthetically beautiful

Cauldron made from sheet metal found as a votive offering
(National Museum of Wales)

and indicative of wealth and power. After 800 BC another industrial phase and a renewed eastern metallurgical link began, reflecting social and political changes (Lynch *et al*).

The development of weaponry was continuous, drawing on influences from the continent and modifications of local technology. In the south, swords were the preferred weapon, while to the north of the Thames spearheads were dominant until after 800 BC, when swords became more widespread. The first British swords were a modification of the rapier—short jabbing swords limited to close-range activity. These were subsequently improved with the advent of a more 'efficient' leaf-shape which did more damage to the human body for the effort expended. Hilts were constantly being refined to increase effectiveness and durability. Scabbards were fitted with chapes that hooked under the left boot to steady the scabbard so that the sword could be drawn while on horseback. Round shields made of leather or wood were probably used in battle, whilst replicas were made of sheet metal some time before 800 BC (Darvill), probably for ceremonial and/or depositional use only, since they were impractical for warfare. The proliferation of weaponry was coincident with the appearance of defensive structures around settlements. The hillforts at Breidden and possibly Ffridd Faldwyn were in use by 1000 BC, the Iron Age not being considered to begin till around 800 BC. This suggests friction between groups, possibly caused by land pressures (Burnham).

Parade weaponry was an important trade during the rise of the warrior aristocracy in the late Bronze Age. There are obvious differences between functional weaponry and parade weaponry, dating back to the over-sized battle-axes and impractical copper daggers of the second millennium. During the Late Bronze Age, this display weaponry became more ornate and impressive, including sinister barbed Broadward spearheads with enormous flat blades (named after a hoard found at Broadward), sheetmetal bronze shields and spectacular, but unwieldy swords.

Metalwork technology may have been more advanced than previously thought. A fascinating artefact was recovered from Bow

Hill, Kingley Vale, Chichester in England. The ceramic object is bowl shaped, with one elongated end and perforated with enough holes that it was thought to be either an oddly shaped sieve, a lantern-cover or a cheese mold. Similar objects had been found in Italy, Sweden, Lithuania, Poland, Hungary and Bavaria, indicating widespread use of this enigmatic yet apparently necessary item. Archaeologist Jacqui Wood tested the item for possible use as

A pottery burner, this one from a late Bronze Age settlement in Poland

a lantern, given the evidence of intense heat on the interior. During these experiments she discovered that when bundles of wax-soaked rushes (a common lamp material in years gone by) were placed inside and lit, a thin, hot flame rose from the centre of the pot, fed by oxygen rushing in from the holes in its sides. These flames could be controlled and maintained for fairly long periods of time, much like a bunsen burner. When the burners were raised on sherds, fuel could be fed in from the bottom, extending burning time indefinitely. Could these have been used for soldering metal or enamelling?

Evidence of pottery is rare, and what exists is usually of poor quality and locally made. Most pottery is found to be of the Deverel Rimbury branch of a broad range of late Bronze Age Welsh pottery. Deverel-Rimbury wares originated in central and southern England around 1200 BC. They were made of local clays, but were stylistically influenced by continental wares and appeared in Montgomeryshire as Beaker use subsided, featuring in both burial and domestic settings. The fabric is gritty and coarse, usually bucket or barrel shaped with simple slashed or perforated decorations. Examples of the barrel shaped type dated to 900 BC were found under the rampart at the Breidden hillfort (Lynch *et al*), and contrast with the elegant bronzework of the then current Wilburton industry and with the sophisticated pottery of the earlier Bronze Age. Evidently, pottery trade and manufacture still suffered from the economic crisis of the late Middle Bronze Age, leaving local communities to draw on their own resources until new trade networks were established in the Iron Age. Yet hints at isolated long-distance contacts are suggested by the discovery of a few sherds of imported flint-tempered and decorated pottery in scattered locations (Lynch *et al*). A recently discovered manufacturing site at Tinney's Lane, Sherborne yielded one of the largest collections of Late Bronze Age pottery in Britain, with over 13,000 sherds. Some sherds may date as far back as the Neolithic, indicating either continued use of the site, deposit of 'antique' ceramics, or re-use of older materials. But the style was post-Deverel Rimbury ware, dating from around 1000 BC to 800 BC. The manufacture took place on a broad terrace measuring 30 by 40 metres, with the clay source at one end. Large, circular discolourations from heat damage on the surface indicates where the firing took place. Fuel was probably provided by straw or gorse, though the evidence is unclear. Enigmatic bullet-shaped clay objects were discovered alongside the pottery, with horizontal holes two-thirds of the way along their length. They may be loomweights. Over 1,200 of these items, all under-fired or otherwise defective, were found deposited in a pit. Molds for metalworking were also manufactured at the site. Several pits and postholes surrounded the area, but the site was evidently solely used for production, probably used seasonally after the pressures of harvesting were over. The remains of a male child were also found in one of the pits, probably of ritual significance and a reminder of the continual association of domestic and ritual life.

Boatmaking was a booming industry of the period, including sea-going as well as lake and river vessels. The cargoes of two sea-going ships were found dating from the Late Bronze Age. The first, dated to 1100 BC was discovered off the coast of Dover and included over 95 bronze objects of continental origin, probably for trade with Britain. The second cargo was discovered off Salcombe and included two palstaves, four blades and a sword.

Competition for resources by a growing population led to greater stress on society and on the landscape. Field systems of larger fields used by one family or group began to be broken down into smaller units, perhaps due to rules of inheritance or prevailing economic issues. Boundaries of scraggly, linear earthworks were established, usually between 3 and 6 metres across and sometimes aligned on barrows or landscape features. Enclosures increased in popularity both for field units and settlements, and enclosed settlements became more common in lowland areas. A mixed economy is evidenced at these sites, with cattle being the most common domestic animal. Rye, a grain able to grow in less favourable conditions, was introduced around this time. From around 1000 BC, settlements of round huts were being constructed on hilltops and slopes, probably to take advantage of a more easily defended position. Breidden in Montgomeryshire, Moel y Gaer and Dinorben, both in Clwyd, were occupied in the 8th century BC, but none were fortified until later.

Chiefdoms formed during the early Bronze Age solidified into powerful political entities by the end of the period. Beginning

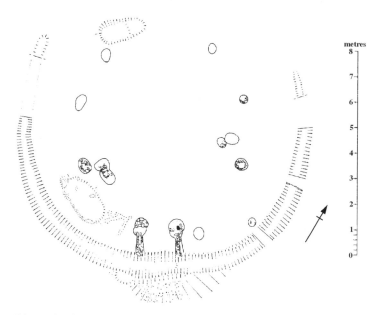

Plan of a hut excavated at Glanfeinion in Montgomeryshire

between 800 BC and 700 BC, small settlements based on familial ties probably formed the basic social unit. These were linked within a broader regional political unit, but it is difficult to determine where the borders of these lay. From within these units, a warrior class was prepared to fight other groups for power and natural resources. The rewards for successful warfare included increased property for the chief, and prestige and material wealth for all of the victors. In this time of the warrior, horsemanship, combat and display were central to the political system. This also included feasting, which appears to have been prevalent; large, sheetmetal cauldrons and buckets used for eating and drinking ceremonies were common throughout Europe during the final Bronze Age.

In western Wales, there is a lack of human evidence for the first third of the first millennium BC. There may have been a settlement hiatus due to the impact of the sub-Atlantic climate with its harsh conditions, but during the later Bronze Age, the population recovered. This increase was probably internally generated rather than augmented by immigration from outside the country (Lynch), as successful adaptation to poorer soils took place and the economy recovered. This period has yielded more evidence of settlements. These were increasingly enclosed and defended as time progressed as people lived under a constant threat of raiding and theft of stores and resources by rival groups. Palisades were developed in northeast Wales, but these were only erected intermittently and then allowed to collapse during periods of minimal threat. Lynch suggests that these defences may have been erected by group leaders as a means of civil control—to provide reassurance and a display of power.

Hillforts began to appear soon after defended settlements, and were probably an offshoot of that technology. With the passing of years defences became stronger and more complex. The conflict and unrest occurring in the Late Bronze Age reached crisis proportions in the northern and central Marches, effecting major changes in social organization (Lynch *et al*), for although hillforts were constructed throughout Wales, the trend appears to originate and proliferate in the Marches. Lynch suggests that the interface between upland and lowland in this area supported a larger population and suffered greater stress as a result. Agricultural yields decreased and the communities relied increasingly upon pastoralism. The constant threat of cattle raiding became an added stress. It is not surprising, therefore, that in addition to the hillfort construction, weapons are found in great numbers (Lynch *et al.*, p.150). Hilltops would have been extremely uncomfortable, cold, windy places to live, indicating that communities were apparently willing to sacrifice convenience for protection (Lynch *et al*).

The use of hillforts varies across Britain. There is evidence in some cases that occupation was periodic, the fort being used as a place of retreat in times of stress. Some hillforts may have been used as political or religious gathering places, where exchange may have taken place with goods being controlled by the elite. Certainly the presence of prestige items in some cases indicates an association with the elite. However, this evidence is scanty (Lynch *et al*). The structures inside the settlement were stone or timber round houses ranging from 7 to 11 metres in diameter. Square or rectangular four-post structures, usually from 2 to 3.5 metres across, were probably storehouses. In some cases these structures were separated within the forts, indicating zoning between residences and other structure types (as at Breidden and Frydd Faldwen, with Moel y Gaer being the best example). There is a general tendency for settlements to be abandoned suddenly, presumably due to the effects of warfare.

Many Welsh settlements from this period were not hillforts, but as most structures were of clay and wood and so highly perishable, scant evidence remains. Their presence is usually revealed by crop-marks and aerial photography, which indicates that the landscape was well populated with huts and fields in the north-west and small, enclosed settlements in the south-west and east (Lynch *et al*), an area that included Montgomeryshire.

Trackways established in the Neolithic and earlier Bronze Age were still in use during the later Bronze Age—indeed, often still are, as with the Kerry Ridgeway in Montgomeryshire. This runs for about 15 miles along a high sandstone ridge between the Severn Valley and the River Teme, striking the crest of the Kerry Hill, and never dipping below 1,000 feet above sea level. The trackway dates from at least the Bronze Age, and perhaps earlier; several Bronze Age monuments are found along the route. The current trackway begins at The Cider House Farm on the B4355 between Newtown and Knighton and ends at Bishop's Castle in Shropshire.

During the Late Bronze Age, horse remains and accoutrements began to appear more frequently in religious settings as horses were considered sacred. A votive deposition at Parc-y-meirch in Denbighshire contained horse bones and bronze horse-fittings of 9th century BC French urnfield origin (Lynch). The White Horse of Uffington, an enormous figure of a horse cut into the chalk of a Berkshire hillside, has been recently redated to between 1400–600 BC.

Change in religious practice is another social transformation resulting from the economic and social crises occurring at the end of the Middle Bronze Age (Bradley, 1998). Graves and grave goods were in decline during this period, as was construction of large monuments, circles and rows. Funereal ceremony lost some of its grandeur, becoming less varied and more low-key. Urned crema-tions became the norm, especially in the lowlands, the vessels used being primarily plain and were placed in the sides and top layers of existing mounds, as at Four Crosses, Welshpool. Some have suggested that the poverty of these burials indicates that they declined in importance. However, ceramic vessels represented a vital part of domestic life and burying a loved one in such a vessel would have been similar to our practice of placing a personal item in the casket of a deceased friend or family member; it serves to create a link between the world of the dead and the world of the living. Additionally, the use of these old mounds indicates a continued belief in their sacredness. Similarly, in some cases burials were placed by older standing stones during the late Bronze and early Iron Ages. Like so many of the new practices, whilst it reflects a modification in the intended use of these monuments, it also shows a continued reverence (Bradley, 1998). Unenclosed Bronze Age flat cemeteries or urnfields are characterized by Deverel-Rimbury ware vessels containing cremated bones. Sometimes the urnfield would have a pre-existing barrow as its central focus and clusters of 10-30 burials are occasionally found within the broader cemetery. These may represent familial units. No evidence of markers remains on the ground surface. Some contend that this indicates continuous, possibly anonymous burials, and others that some type of surface markers probably existed, but have been destroyed over time.

There are only nine possible Welsh examples of Late Bronze Age metalwork accompanying burials, one of them in the Breidden Hills where the burial was accompanied by metal tools, weaponry and some personal ornamentation.

As the practice of burials declined during the 9th and 8th centuries BC, so that of votive depositions reached its peak. These depositions are increasingly associated with water, although they are often found on land, perhaps beneath a marker or older monument. These deposits consist of varied objects of value, perhaps offerings to deities. Objects found in such depositions may span many years, suggesting that sites were re-used continually for these ceremonies. The objects are usually of great value and have been deliberately broken, so continuing the ancient tradition of placing broken pottery sherds and domestic implements in pits, graves, and at entrances and post-holes of large monuments. There is some question and current debate as to whether hoards, traditionally

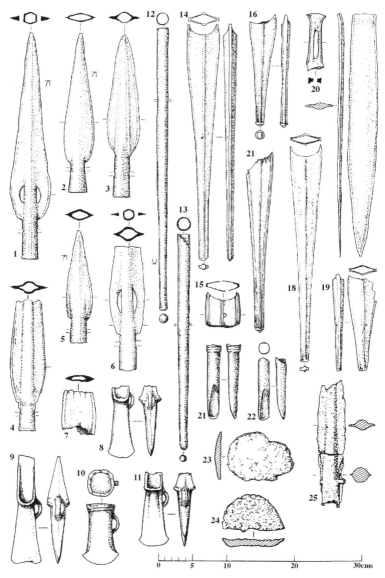

Selection of items found at Guilsfield Hoard: 1-7 Spears;
8, 9, 11 Palstaves; 10 Socketed axe; 11, 12 Spear ferrules;
14, 15, 16, 19 Scabbard sheath ends, one rectangular-shaped, rest
tongue-shaped; 20 hilt and blade of Wilburton-style sword;
21, 22 Socketed gouges; 23, 24 ingots; 25 faulty spear casting

thought to be a secular phenomenon, may also have a symbolic meaning.

A renewed interest in natural sanctuaries such as lakes, rivers and perhaps sacred trees appears in the last centuries of the Bronze Age. The concern with water was not a new one, for ceremonial monuments of preceding periods were frequently located near the source of rivers and along streams. The location of a fine artefact like the Bryncir lunula—a beaten gold neck ornament discovered in a peat bog at Bryncir (Caernarfonshire)—is another indication of the importance of watery areas. Then again, the increase of votive deposits in bogs and rivers coincides with the decrease in burials, leading some to suggest that depositions may have had funereal associations. The presence of human bones in proximity to these deposits certainly lends credence to this suggestion, and it may be that the 'missing' burial evidence from this period is because most of it still lies underwater. Certainly, evidence for burial is rare for this period in Montgomeryshire, reflecting the overall British trend (Arnold), Four Crosses yielding the only examples in the county. Here, three urns of late Bronze Age type were found inserted into one barrow, in keeping with the practice of earlier barrow ceme-teries in other areas, and another possible burial is suggested by urn fragments found in a second barrow (Arnold).

In the guise of a purely religious act, votive offerings would have reflected a chief's prestige and willingness to sacrifice his valuable items for the greater good, emphasizing his role as a provider for the people. It has been suggested that such sacrifice may have been a means of resolving rivalries between chiefs, as a means of equalizing wealth between citizens and groups, thus temporarily calming stress in this increasingly competitive envi-ronment (Bradley, 1998, 137-9).

Montgomeryshire yields much evidence of hoarding in keeping with the countrywide obsession with this practice during the late Bronze Age. Metalwork of the Wilburton/Wallington phase is found in the large Guilsfield and Buttington Hall hoards as well as in stray finds (Arnold). The Guilsfield hoard was found near the Gaer Fawr Hillfort in Guilsfield, Montgomeryshire, its contents all of the Wilburton Complex type, dating from 1500 BC. This industry, focused in the south-east of England, is characterized by imported copper ore from central Europe, to which a large amount of lead was added, allowing for thinner castings. Spearheads and broad, leaf-shaped swords were the most common products. The Guilsfield hoard yielded 120 pieces including spearheads, some of distinctive hollow-bladed and lunate opening types; broad sword blades; tongue chapes (scabbard covers), and straight spear ferrules. Local tools including gouges and light, narrow-bladed palstaves were found alongside the weapons. These objects represent the greatest variety of any hoard found in Wales, and the exclusivity of this type of metalwork to the Severn Valley may be related to the exclusivity of Welsh late Bronze Age hillforts to this area. A small hoard from Llanrhaeadr-ym-Mochnant yielded Wilburton /Wallington phase socketed gouges. Another interesting hoard found at Llanrhaiadr-ym-Mochnant yielded nine torcs.

Craig y Llyn Ridge Monuments

This group consist of several cairns, two standing stones, a stone row, two stone circles
Location: 8 miles west-north-west of Newtown
Access: Most lie alongside public footpaths

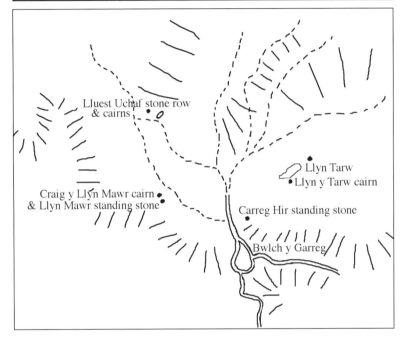

To reach a base point for this group of sites, head west from Newtown on the A489. Turn right onto the A470 and pass through Caersws. Having passed under the railway line turn right on the lane that heads north toward Bwlch y Garreg. Park towards the end of this lane.

Carreg Hir Standing Stone

(SO 014 969)

To reach this stone, take the path through the gate across from Lluest y Greolen. Follow the path north-east and the stone will become apparent to you immediately, to the left of the path approximately 100 metres along.

Carreg Hir, a large standing stone measuring 1.6 metres high by 1.1 metres wide and 0.8 metres thick, is located on a south facing slope, with its long axis aligned south-west to north-east, overlooking valleys and mountains on three sides. Smaller stones clustered at the base probably represent modern interference. The monument lies along an ancient bridleway leading from between Llyn Du and Llyn Mawr to Llyn-y-Tarw, and possibly represents a marker. Carreg Hir, like most British standing stones is associated with other monuments. The Llyn Tarw ringcairn (not to be confused with the Llyn y Tarw cairn detailed below) is located just beyond the skyline but is very difficult to find.

Craig y Llyn Mawr Cairn

(SO 002 972)

Go through the cattle gate on the left of the road near Lluest y Greolen. Follow the path north-west between the lakes. Paths diverge at the foot of the ridge and you follow the path to the left $^1/8$ of a mile across the pasture. The cairn can be seen directly past a gate.

This round cairn is located on a south-west facing slope near the southern terminal end of Craig y Llyn Mawr ridge. The cairn measures 0.6 metres high by 8 metres in diameter. A robbing pit found in the north-west quadrant measures 1.5 metres by 1 metre. The south-west and south-east quadrants are surrounded by a 4-metre wide possible ditch. The site overlooks Llyn Mawr and Llyn Ddu to the south and an expansive valley to the west.

See also the entry for the Llyn Mawr standing stone on page 106.

Lluest Uchaf Stone Row and Cairns

(SO 001 983)

This is a long, difficult walk requiring stout hiking boots, a head covering (to withstand strong winds), sunscreen and provisions including water and a light snack. The hike will take upwards of an hour. Go through the gate at the end of the road and follow the path north-west for approximately 1 mile. You will pass Lluestuchaf cottage. The climb is steep and the walk is difficult. Keep going along the path. The stone row is located at the farthest end of the craig, facing north.

Lluest Uchaf, Caersws is a single row of 11 stones running 12 metres north to south on the southern, downward-sloping terminal end of a ridge which marks the highest point in the immediate land-scape, overlooking the ritual landscape below. The tallest stone is 0.5 metres high. The row is aligned with the craig, forming what appears to be an extension of the natural feature. The longer axes of all except the centre stone are aligned with the row, with the south-ernmost stone being just slightly off alignment. The central stone's longer side is perpendicular to the row's alignment, and has large stones piled around the base. The monument overlooks a valley to the west, east and north with the view extending to the mountains beyond, a placement that gives one the impression that the monu-ment is on a dome at the centre of a large natural circle.

The row is aligned with two cairns located directly to the north and lower down the slope. The first is a round cairn covered with turf that measures 10 metres in diameter and 0.3 metres high. Stone is visible on the south, west and north sides of the cairn. The second cairn is oval, also covered in turf, and measures 5 metres north to south by 4 metres east to west and stands 0.3 metres high. The cairn is bounded on its long axis by shallow ditches 1 metre wide. Surface stones are visible on the west side.

Llyn Mawr Standing Stone

(SO 002 972)

Go through the gate on the left of the road near Lluest y Greolen and follow the path north-west between the lakes. The paths diverge at the foot of the ridge and follow the path to the left for $^1/_8$ of a mile. The standing stone is directly before the gate. Two cairns can be seen directly past the gate (for one of which see page 103).

The Llyn Mawr standing stone is located at the head of Llyn Mawr on the lower slopes at the southern terminal end of the Craig y Llyn Mawr ridge (CPAT 609). The stone is surrounded by a small Bronze Age cairn. The monument measures 1.35 metres high, 0.6 metres long and 0.3 metres thick. This stone is along the same route as Carreg Hir and several cairns in close proximity.

Llyn Tarw Ritual Complex
Llyn Tarw Circle

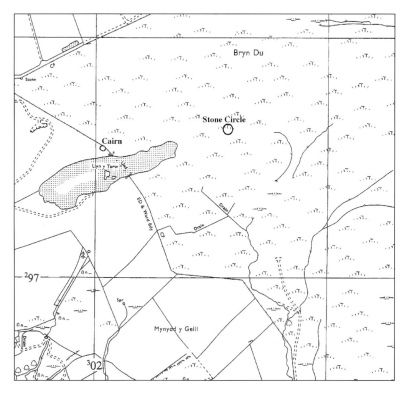

(SO 026 976)

Go through the gate directly ahead of you at the end of the lane and follow the bridleway for approximately half a mile. Then turn right onto the path toward Llyn Tarw, turning left on the lakeside path, going east. Follow the path around the head of the lake. The circle is located 100 metres across the grass east of the lakehead. The circle is very difficult to see, as none of the stones stand over the bracken. A GPS device may be necessary to see this site.

Llyn-y-Tarw I stone circle is sited on a level terrace of a south-east facing slope 200 metres north-east of Llyn y Tarw. The circle is 19.25 metres in diametre comprises 39 visible stones. More stones are probably buried in the peat. If spacing is regular, the circle probably comprised 90 stones. All the stones are of local origin and range from being barely above ground level to standing 39 centimetres high. A cairn is located just outside the circle to the south-west; a total of eight cairns have been recorded in the vicinity.

Llyn-y-Tarw II, 13 metres in diameter, comprises 10 small, low stones. The possible remains of a cairn was found in the centre. This circle also lay on a small terrace, but it can no longer be seen. The area surrounding these circles contains many edge-set stones, cairns and other possible monuments.

Y Capel is located 3.5 kilometres to the north-west and may be associated with the Llyn-y-Tarw complex as the area between them is crowded with Bronze Age monuments (Dorling). The view from the monument overlooks the upper Severn Valley and the distant Breidden hills.

Llyn y Tarw Cairn

(SO021974)

The cairn is located 10 metres north of the lake on the fence line immediately to the south of the point where the bridleway crosses it.

A small stony burial mound 7.6 metres in diameter and 0.7 metres high, the cairn has a smooth profile with a flattish top. There are exposed stones visible, particularly around the outside. The monument may be a 'kerb cairn', due to the possible evidence of a surrounding kerb or low stone wall, though little evidence remains of this.

Carneddau Barrows

Structured Cairns with earthen elements
Location: 1¹/₂ miles north-east of Carno (SN 992 996)
Access: Public footpath leads past the cairns on open hillside

From Newtown take the A489 west, then turn right onto the A470 to Caersws. Continue on to Carno and about quarter of a mile beyond the post office on the right, turn right on the road signposted to Llanfair Caereinion. After about half a mile, turn right onto the narrow lane marked with a 'T' no through road sign. Continue along until, just past a farm on the left, the road turns to the left and gains a stoned rather than tarmac surface. You want to park near this point.

Walk back down towards the farm, and then take the public foot-path into the field on the left that crosses into the next field between two posts, carries on up the hillside on the same line, then swings round (and becomes more visible on the ground in due course) to shadow the deep valley on your left, The path swings left at the top of this valley then climbs the hillside between the two woodlands, in due course technically heading over to shadow the woodland on the right up the hillside. When you reach the fence that runs between the two pieces of woodland, cross through the gate that will leave the fence that carries on along towards the crest of the ridge on your left. Shadow this fence towards the top and you will reach the cairns.

Carneddau I and II ring cairns date from approximately 2500 through to 1200 BC and are contemporary with larger ritual complexes in the area. Excavation has revealed that a nearby timber circle was added around 1900 BC forming a sacred landscape sited with the Breidden hills. The first phase, a cairn 7 metres in diam-eter surrounded by a circle of large, loose stones 5 metres wide overlies a rectangular cist located in the central area. The cist, measuring 1.24 metres long, 0.44 metres wide and 0.4 metres deep, contained an unaccompanied secondary cremation for which the primary burial had been removed to make room. This is evidenced by the fragments of cremated human bone and crushed early Bronze Age pottery scattered in the covering material and around the cist. There is evidence for regular sepulchro-ritual activities in this central area, including the on-site defleshing of corpses prior to cremation. This activity is essentially a Neolithic tradition that was evidently still upheld in this part of Wales. A nearby hearth yielded burnt remains of an early Bronze Age archer's stone wristguard. This hearth was used on several occasions during the life of the monument and may have provided the layer of charcoal from a fire made during the time of construction that was laid in a circle around the central area. The cairn was constructed over this layer. The charcoal was also used to seal the cremation pits.

In total, the stone ring contained four cists. The easternmost cist was empty but the acids may have destroyed the inhumation. The western cist contained a cremation accompanied by a flint knife and flake. The south-eastern cist was probably the latest in the series of burials and contained a broken Food Vessel and fragments of cremated bone. The other cist contained a cremation in an inverted Collared Urn, one of the largest of its type found in Wales. Inverted urn burials became common practice during the Middle Bronze Age — a burial at Lan Fawr comprising an inverted urn placed over the cremation of a two-year-old child has been dated to 1600 BC. It has been suggested by Richard Bradley that overturned urns may represent roundhouses, classic domestic structures of the time.

A satellite cairn was added to the northern arc of the main site which covered a cremation pit containing over a kilo of cremated bone. Within the arc that extends north-west to north-east, the maximum rising and setting points of the midsummer sun, there is evidence of pyro-ritual activity. This emphasis on the northern arc reflects cardinal point orientation of contemporary stone circles such as Y Capel, 1 km to the east.

Hazelnut shells were found in pits and in the cairn ring (Gibson, 1989).

Trannon Moor Ritual Complex

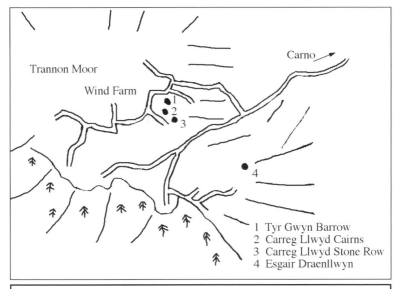

1 Tyr Gwyn Barrow
2 Carreg Llwyd Cairns
3 Carreg Llwyd Stone Row
4 Esgair Draenllwyn

Various Cairns and Stone Row
Location: 3 miles west of Carno
Access: On hillside with a variety of access roads and footpaths,
although some 'bog-trotting' can be required!

From Newtown, head west on the A489, turning right onto the A470 and pass through Caersws. Just beyond the post office and stores in Carno (and just before a stretch of stone wall alongside the A470 on the left) make a left turn by the house named Gwynfa. Stay on the 'main' minor road as it winds west. As you head out onto the open hillside you will pass the Carno Windfarm Service centre on the left. The road will turn to a gravelled track, and after a few hundred yards on this, park just before the gate beyond which only authorised vehicles are permitted.

Carreg Llwyd, Stone Row

(SN 920 957)

Walk on along the track from where you parked. When you're adjacent to the path that leads to the second wind turbine on the left, to your right you should be able to see a stile that crosses the fence on the skyline of the ridge; about 50 yards to its right is a large stone that marks the end of the stone row. The easiest way to reach the stile, is to start on the path that leads to the next wind turbine on the right of the track, then pick your way across the hillside to the stile.

Carreg Llwyd stone row is sited on a slope below the horizon and comprises 17 stones terminating in a large recumbent stone at the southernmost end. Orientation is north to south. The large terminal stone measures 3 metres long by 1 metre square at its broader end. It is unknown whether this stone ever stood upright.

There are currently two rows, spaced about 1 metre apart with 6 stones in the eastern row and 11 in the western row. Stones from the western row measures up to 0.4 metres high and 1.5 to 0.8 metres long. Excavation in 2000 proved that rather than being a double row, the monument is a single row whose alternating stones collapsed in opposite directions. Along with several cairns and standing stones in the area Carreg Llwyd comprises a ritual landscape. The landscape is made surreal by the presence of a large windfarm.

Carreg Llwyd Cairns

(SN 919 957)

You can see the associated stone row (see previous entry) to the right from the gravel road, and initially follow the directions to reach the row. Walk due north 150 metres. The cairns are at the top of the slope, but not that obvious to find.

The more southerly of the pair is a kerb cairn measuring 6 metres in diameter by 0.5 metres high and is composed of slabs up to 1.6 metres long and 0.5 metres high. A scatter of small stones lies in the centre. The more northerly of the pair is a kerb cairn measuring 5 metres in diameter by 0.5 metres high, and is composed of slabs 1.5 metres long by 0.5 metres high. A recumbent stone 1 metre square lies in the centre. The third is a ring cairn 18 metres in diameter with a stone bank 2 metres wide and 0.3 metres high. The central open area inside the bank measures 13 metres in diameter and has an entrance to the south-east. A central cist measures 1 metre square. An internal orthostatic kerb (*i.e.* made of large upright stones) was discovered around the north-east quadrant of the third cairn, which was previously interpreted as a small domestic structure.

Tyr Gwyn Round Cairn

(SN 918 961)

Once again, initially follow the directions to the stone row. Tyr Gwyn is very visible beyond the row, its pile of stones being split by the fence that runs away from you across the moor.

Tyr Gwyn dominates the sites on Trannon Moor and is located midway between two main valleys. A large and prominent rubble cairn, Tyr Gwyn measures 26 metres in diameter and 1.5 metres high, whilst a central pit measures 6 metres in diameter. The cairn has been disturbed by a fence and a sheepfold built across it.

Esgair Draenllwyn Stone Setting

(SN 931 951)

From where you parked you need to walk along the track, keeping left, and then shadowing the woodland that's on your right, turning left onto the track that services four wind turbines (and reached just before the last wind turbine close to the wood is reached). Alternatively, pick up this track if heading over from the other sites on Trannon Moor.

From the last of the four turbines walk up to the fence and then follow this across the hillside to the promontory (for a distance that is about one and a half times the distance between the last two turbines). The setting is on the promontory.

This stone setting is rather confusing and difficult to interpret as two alignments seem to be at work. The first, a north-west to south-east alignment, comprises three edge-set stones of which the middle stone has its axis set at right angles to the alignment. The stones are also unevenly spaced—the middle stone is 10 metres from the south-east one and 3 metres from the north-west one. A small cairn is found 3 metres from the row, and another standing stone is located 5 metres south-west of the central stone of the row and sharing its axial alignment. Around 5 metres from the north-west stone is another upright with its axis aligned north-east to south-west.

117

Glog Hill Barrows

Group of Barrows
Location: 3 miles south of Newtown (SO 087 851,
089 852, 091 852, 091 854, 092 854, 093 854, 097 855, 098 854,
096 855)
Access: Via public and permissive footpaths

This is a steep climb on the footpath but well worth the effort. The path has some thoughtfully placed seats on which to regain your breath if so needed. From Newtown head south on the A483. Pass through Dolfor and the junction with the B4355 and after about another mile initially pass Cefn Lea campsite on the right and then Glog Farm is reached on the left. Park near here. (You may wish to return to the lay-by opposite Cefn Lea to park).

Walk up the farm road whch is also the footpath up the hillside, turning diagonally to the left in the yard to reach the track signposted 'to top of mountain'. This zig-zags up to the crest, just before which you turn right to enter the area of barrows. The path ends at the burial monuments.

Glog Hill comprises at least eight barrows in this upland area of pasture and moorland, a further three could be natural in origin since the landscape is so uneven. The main monument is a large Bronze Age barrow or cairn located on the highest point of a ridge and measures 16 metres in diameter by 1.5 metres high. This mound is signposted for easy recognition (see photo opposite). A second mound is located across the pasture, has an OS pillar on the top and can be accessed by a trackway leading directly to it. This mound is 20 metres in diameter and 2 metres high. A third distinguishable mound can be found in the same pasture as the second and measures 23 metres in diameter by 3 metres high.

From Glog Hill, Kerry Two Tumps to the east and Caebetin to the north-east are intervisible as dominant features of the skyline. All three monuments are located at significant Mid-Wales points lying between sources of important waterways. The view from Glog Hill is spectacular, overlooking the valley and distant mountains on three sides. This location once again gives the impression that the monument is on a dome rising out of the valley and stands at the centre of an immense natural circle.

Kerry Hill Stone Circle

Stone Circle
Location: 4 miles south of Newtown (SO 157 861)
Access: Located 50 metres off a public footpath

From Newtown: take the A489 east toward Kerry. In the village turn right onto the B4368. Follow it uphill and right on the Welsh/English border, take a very sharp left up a steep, narrow road. (If you reach the Anchor pub you've gone just too far.) Follow this road for approximately half a mile up to the Kerry Pole (a large pole with a small metal fox on top of it on your left) at the top of the hill. This is the Kerry Ridgeway. Park by the small abandoned house on the right.

Walk through the cattle gate on the left side (the Kerry Pole side) of the road and follow the path west to the first fence. Go through the cattle gate and continue west on to the second fence. Go through the gate and take a left, walking south along the fence. When you get to the end of the fence, take a right. Walk west along the fence approximately 50 metres to reach the circle.

Kerry Hill Circle is known locally as the Druid Stones. Set on a gentle south-western slope, this circle is one of the largest in the area at 26.5 metres in diameter. The monument comprises nine very regularly spaced stones set 10 metres apart (with one current exception), together with a central stone. The stones, all of sandstone, are fairly small ranging from 0.3 to 0.5 metres high. Two of these outer stones form a pair, although one is fallen (Burnham), and are set tangentially to the circle. A large flat stone 1.4 metres long lies recumbent at the centre of the circle. Traces of a bank remain at the northern arc, but this may be the result of grazing damage (CPAT 609). Again, views are spectacular. The Nant Rhyd y Fedw valley is seen to the south and west with mountains visible in the distance.

Stone Dimensions:

Central Stone: 0.35 x 0.5 x 1.3 metres, recumbent.

Beginning with stone 1 on the west:

1. Recumbent, 1.05 x 0.4 x 0.17 metres; some erosion of turf around base caused by livestock.
2. Recumbent, 0.9 x 0.5 x 0.16 metres; flat regular-shaped stone with modern inscriptions.
3. Upright, 0.6 x 0.35 x 0.2 metres; disturbance caused by livestock around base, irregularly shaped.
4. Upright, 0.4 x 0.25 x 0.15 metres; irregularly shaped.
5. Recumbent, 0.87 x 0.8 x 0.4 metres – irregularly shaped.
6. Upright but leaning, 0.45 x 0.12 x 0.25 metres.
7. Upright but leaning, 0.55 x 0.55 x 0.25 meters, and is currently set right behind stone 6. It is likely that has been moved from its original poistion.
8. 0.8 x 0.3 x 0.45 metres.
9. Recumbent, 0.47 x 0.36 x 0.1 metres.

Two Tumps Barrows

Two Barrows
Location: 4 miles south of Newtown (SO 117 851)
Access: Lie alongside a public bridleway

From Newtown take the A483 south. In Dolfor turn left onto the B4365. As this climbs up the hill you reach a newly created parking area on the left (a few hundred yards before you reach a house called the Cider House on maps and a small piece of woodland on the right). The bridleway has recently been extended down the side of the road to this parking area.

Walk up the bridleway, turning left opposite the Cider House on to the old route. Continue for approximately 0.4 miles. Two Tumps is directly past an earthen dyke.

Kerry Two Tumps comprises two tumuli located on a peak along the Kerry Ridgeway on the western end of the Kerry Hills near a dyke. The mounds are aligned with the ridgeway, north-east / south-west. The westernmost barrow measures 24.5 metres in diameter and 1.7 metres high, has a flat top and contained one inhumation and three cremations within the barrow. The eastern barrow measures 24 metres in diameter and around 1 metre high and contained a single cremation. This monument is intervisible with Glog Hill and Caebetin and forms a prominent ritual skyline. There are splendid valley and mountain views on all sides.

Ceffig Gaerau Stone Circle

Stone Circle
Location: 14 miles north-west of Newtown (SH 903 005)
Access: Right alongside a public footpath

From Newtown head west on the 489, and turn right onto the A470. Go through Caersws and Carno and turn left in Tallerdig, on the road signposted to Bont Dolgadfan. Continue for about 1½ miles, and just past the second road to your left and as the road starts to descend downhill, there is a footpath signposted off to the right through a farm gate. Park near here.

Follow the footpath, which turns right at the base of the hill, then passes through a gate into a field and shadows a small piece of woodland on the right, before turning left and takes a more obvious form) and shadowing the gully on your right up the hillside. At the top, the path crosses one fence by a stile, and the stone circle is right beside the path where it reaches the next stile.

This stone circle is 22 metres in diameter and comprises eight recumbent stones which lie in livestock-worn hollows on moorland (see plan of layout overleaf). The stones are unevenly spaced and meaure between 1.2 and 2.0 metres. In the central area is a hollow,

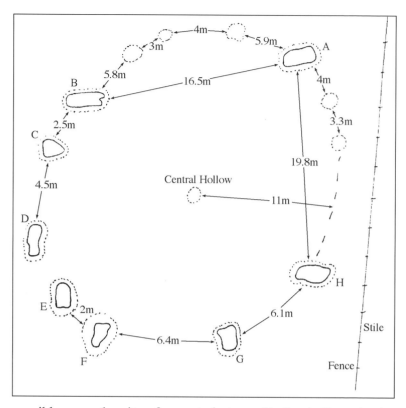

possibly once the site of a central stone. Similar hollows in the circumference of the circle possibly represent missing stones. The circle is situated close to the Yr Allor cairn and Lled-croen-yr-ych stone circle (see next entries).

Lled-croen-yr-ych Stone Circle

Stone Circle
Location: 14 miles north-west of Newtown (SH 903 006)
Access: Close to a public footpath

Follow the directions as for the previous entry, the stone circle lying 40 metres to the right of the path once you have crossed the stile that is beside the Ceffig Gaerau stone cirle.

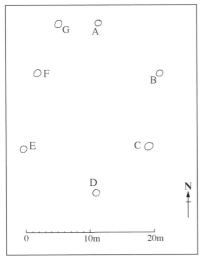

This circle comprises five stones with two outlying stones immediately to the north-west. The stones have in some cases been moved. The stones stand upright in animal-worn hollows in which some dumping of small stones has taken place. The circle measures 26 metres in diameter and stands in the centre of a field in close proximity to the Yr Allor cairn (see next entry) and the Ceffig Gaerau stone circle (see previous entry).

Yr Allor Cairn

Cairn
Location: 14 miles north-west of Newtown (SH 898 004)
Access: Located a few hundred yards off a public footpath, from
which it is nevertheless very visible

Follow the instructions for reaching the Ceffig Gaerau stone cirle.
From this circle, if you look to the crest of the hillside to the west
(*i.e.* the left as you climbed up), on the far side of the fence and
right on the skyline you'll see the outline of Yr Allor Cairn.

This is a large round cairn on the peak of Newydd Fynyddog,
the highest peak in the area, and is intervisible with Ceffig Gaerau
and Lled-croen-yr-ych stone circles to the east. Measuring 14
metres east to west and 13 metres north to south, the cairn consists
of a circle of large stones with smaller boulders inside and in
between the larger stones. All these elements were constructed
upon a foundational circle of stones 15 metres in diameter. This
circle is still visible in places, but has been seriously compromised
by human, animal and weather damage. The largest stone is 2

metres in length. A hollow left by excavation or robbing measures
1 metre in depth; an excavation carried out in 1860 suggests that the
cairn held a cist with skeletal remains.

The cairn has been seriously tampered with, a windbreak having
been built on the southern side. However, it is still well worth the
hike up the mountain. The view is spectacular, overlooking valleys
on all sides and the mountains in the distance. The monument sits
on a dome rising out out of the valley and surrounded by distant
mountains. The impression is gained that one is standing at the
cosmic centre of a very large circle.

Ffridd yr Ystrad Cairns

A group of three cairns and a standing stone
Location: 13 miles north-west of Newtown (SN 918 990)
Access: A public footpath leads up onto the hillside on which the
monuments lie, but is in a poor state of repair. The area around
the cairns themselves has been recently fenced

From Newtown head west on the 489, and turn right onto the A470.
Go through Caersws and Carno and turn left in Tallerdig, on the
road signposted to Bont Dolgadfan. After about a mile, take what is
the first left off this road and park at its very end at Cwm-cach-
Uchaf.

A footpath in a poor state of access leads up the hillside behind
the farm starting to the right of the farm building. It soon swings
left and then right to run into a fence. Across this it continues up the
hillside. The cairns themselves are situated on the promontory of
the hill to your left as you climb up.

Theree cairns are separated by distances of up to 180 metres and
due to the undulating nature of the upland landscape are not all
intervisible. The three cairns are dissimilar in appearance partly due

to disturbance to their environment which has affected two of them. The most westerly has an exposed stone lined burial cist and the central cairn has a hole at its centre, possibly the result of robbing. The third, most southerly cairn, appears to be intact and undisturbed. A small standing stone has been erected close to the central cairn.

Cairn 1 (PRN4303) SN 920 990: Located just to the north of the modern fence line. The cairn is visible as a grassed-over mound 6 metres in diameter and 0.4 metres high. There are some stones on the surface but it is mostly grassed over. The CPAT probed the mound and found it to be intact and stony beneath the turf cover, with no indications that the cairn has ever been disturbed.

Cairn 2 (PRN4305) SN 917 990: This is the most visually impressive of the three cairns on account of the well constructed stone lined cist which lies exposed at its centre (see photo opposite). Overall the cairn measures 8 metres in diameter and 0.5 metres high at the centre. The cist measures 0.9 by 0.6 metres and is 0.3 metres deep. The cist is lined with four stone slabs. No capstone is present.

Cairn 3 (PRN9189) SN 919 991: This cairn has a standing stone beside it. Of the three it is the most battered. Today it measures 7 x 5.5 metres and 0.3 metres tall. At the centre there is a hole 2 metres across and 0.2 metres deep with some stones inside it.

The standing stone (PRN4307): 0.7 metres high and 0.7 x 0.2 metres in size is located close to the third cairn.

Llanrhaeadr ym Mochnant
Ritual Complex

The extensive Llanrhaeader ym Mochnant ritual landscape
comprises two stone circles, a stone row a henge, two pit circles,
a cairn and a standing stone. The henge may date from the Late
Neolithic while the remaining monuments probably represent
Bronze Age activity.
Location: Near the spectacular Pystll Rhaider falls
Access: Most lie alongside public footpaths

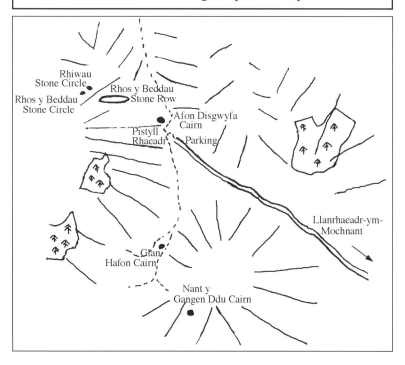

To reach the complex, take the A490 north from Welshpool to Coed
y Llan. Turn right onto the B4391 and after about 300 yards, bear
right at the fork onto the B4580 northbound. This will take you into
the village of Llanrhaeadr ym Mochnant. Bear left and right in the
village, following signs for Pistyll Rhaeadr falls, and park in the
carpark near the foot of the falls.

Afon Disgynfa Cairn

(SJ 070 297)

From the car park, take the footpath to the top of the falls. At the top of the falls, follow the stream northwest into the fields. The cairn lies on a western facing slope 3.5 kilometres across the field.

This is a stony round cairn measuring 15 metres in diameter and standing to 1 metre in height with a central hollow 2 metres wide by 0.9 metres deep. The cairn is located just north of the main footpath which leads from the waterfall westwards towards the stone circle, and is clearly visible due to its size. It is built of many stones and may include a series of single stones around the northern arc. The hollow may be a result of stones being moved to create a shelter, rather than robbing, and probably does not extend to the bottom of the cairn.

Rhos-y-Beddau Stone Row

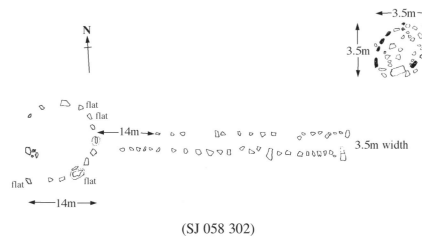

(SJ 058 302)

From the car park, take the footpath to the top of the falls. At the top of the falls, follow the stream northwest into the fields. The monuments are located approximately 1 mile across the fields, at the divergence of the stream into two streamlets.

Rhos-y-Beddau is the longest and most famous stone row in the area, but is barely visible above the vegetation. The monument runs 60 metres on a west to east axis, stopping 8 metres short of the Rhos-y-Beddau stone circle. The double row is aligned along the valley, pointing to its head. As the rows near the stone circle, they converge from 4 metres to 2 metres apart. The easternmost 12 metres of the row has a slightly different alignment suggesting a separate phase of construction. The stones of the northern row, comprising 12 remaining stones, are smaller than the 24 remaining stones in the southern row. The avenue is associated, though not aligned, with a small cairn, seen as a slight rise in the ground to the north (CPAT 609). The cairn is probably a ring cairn, though it is much disturbed and difficult to evaluate.

Rhos-y-Beddau and Cwm Rhiwiau Stone Circles

(Rhos-y-Beddau SJ 058 302; Cwm Rhiwiau SJ 060 306)
From the car park, take the footpath to the top of the falls. At the top of the falls, follow the stream northwest into the fields. The monuments are located approximately 1 mile across the fields, at the divergence of the stream into two streamlets.

Rhos-y-Beddau and Cwm Rhiwiau are two closely related circles. Rhos-y-Beddau measures 12 metres in diameter (see plan opposite) and is situated on a natural terrace within an upland valley leading from Llanrhaeadr to the Berwyn ridge, overlooking the confluence of the Afon Disgynfa and Nant-y-Llyn rivers. There are 12 stones still visible in the circle with a gap in the northwest arc. The stones are very low, barely visible above the vegetation, the largest being 0.6 metres high, typical of the area's stone circles (CPAT 609). A large quartz boulder is associated with the monument and may have ritual significance.

Cwm Rhiwiau is an egg-shaped stone 'circle' on a plateau 400 metres north of Rhos-y-Beddau on the north bank of a stream. The setting measures 11.4 metres north-south by 10.4 metres east-west. The stones are small, ranging from 0.12 to 0.4 metres high, the largest measuring 0.37 tall by 0.57 metres wide. An outlying stone can be found 1.3 metres to the north and another 20 metres to the south. These are roughly aligned with Rhos-y-Beddau and probably indicate celestial orientation of the monument.

Nant y Gangen Ddu Cairn

(SJ 075 268)

From the car park, take the footpath to the top of the falls. At the top of the falls, take the footpath due south approximately 2 kilometres. The monument is on the left side of the path.

Nant y Gangen Ddu round cairns can be found on the southern slope of Glan Hafon.

The most northerly of the pair is a turf covered cairn measuring 8 metres in diameter by 0.4 metres high. There is a turfed-over pit measuring 1 metre square by 0.2 metres deep in the south-west quadrant. A scatter of stones across the north-west quadrant may come from the cairn itself. There are indications of a former kerb at the southern and south-eastern edge.

The southern of the pair is a partially turf-covered round cairn measuring 10 metres in diameter by 0.5 metres high and contains a cist in the northwest quadrant, measuring 1.3 by 1.1 metres by 0.2 metres deep. A field bank, 1.5 metres wide by 0.5 metres high curves around the northern edge of the cairn, covered by a heap of rubble.

Glan Hafon Cairn

(SJ 071 276)

From the car park, take the footpath to the top of the falls. At the top of the falls, take the footpath due south approximately 3 kilometres. The monument is on the right side of the path.

Glan Hafon is a turf-covered cairn measuring 10 metres in diameter and 0.5 metres high. A massive boulder sits in the centre measuring 2 metres high and 3 metres in diameter, which some interpret as a symbolic capstone. The cairn is located at the head of Cwm Nant Ddial on the col between Glan Hafon and Y Cogydd. The view is spectacular, overlooking the Dyffryn Tanat to the south and west.

Cerrig yr Helfa Stone Row

Stone Row
Location: 15 miles west of Welshpool (SH 983 156)
Access: By the side of a forestry track, itself reached
by public footpath

From Welshpool take the A458 west. In Foel, and almost opposite the shop, turn right. Fork right after about 1½ miles by the public telephone box (and shortly before you would otherwise have crossed the stream in the valley bottom). Continue past one farm on the roadside, and then a second which lies down a track to the left and park by the third which is on the right of the road. This is Pen-y-coed farm.

The public footpath goes through the set of farm buildings, passing immediately alongside the wall of a newer building. Once on the track beyond, head towards the ridge in the field, bearing left at the foot of the ridge on the track which curves around the ridge to reach the edge of the forestry beyond. Go through the gate here, and walk up the path to the new forestry road. Keep straight ahead at all the junctions, heading into the forestry, and after about half a mile you reach a quarry on the left-hand side. Stay on the forestry road straight ahead and after about 300 yards the stone row is found in area of grassland on the right of the track.

Today the Cerrig yr Helfa stone row comprises ten stones, but it is thought that some stones may be missing as there are several gaps in the construction. A slight depression scattered with fragments of quartz suggests that there may have been a burial pit or cist in the centre of the monument, a traditional practice at stone rows throughout Wales.

Stone 2 (the second stone from the north) is not in its original position, though it is part of the original monument, Gibson postulating that it was part of the central cist or pit and a corresponding stone is found lying on its edge next to the central depression. Stone 1 may have been part of the central monument as well, as its position is slightly offset from the others in the row. (CPAT 24)

Stone Dimensions:
1. 0.5 x 0.38 x 0.58 m high (northernmost stone)
2. 0.5 x 0.2 x 0.95 m (modern addition)
3. 0.16 x 0.10 x 0.08 m
4. 0.44 x 0.12 x 0.08 m
5. 1.4 x 0.5 x 0.6 (damaged during felled)
6. 0.7 x 0.3 x 0.44 m (forms close set pair)
7. 0.6 x 0.6 x 0.8 m (not in original position)
8. 1.7 x 0.4 x 2 m (not in original position)
9. 0.28 x 0.3 x 0.08 m
10. 0.56 x 0.24 x 0.34 m (southernmost stone)

Carnedd das Eithen Barrow

Barrow
Location: 14 miles north-west of Welshpool (SJ 051 238)
Access: On open hillside, not easily reached by public footpaths

The barrow lies on the slopes above Cwm Hirnant on the road leading to Lake Vyrnwy from Penybontfawr in the Tanat Valley.

Carnedd das Eithen's significance is emphasized by its mountaintop location on the summit of Y Das Eithin and its dominance over the horizon. Some patterning can be discerned in upland barrow distribution. In this area there are several cairns found on ridges, crests and hill and mountaintops.

The cairn measures 20 metres in diameter and is 1.8 metres high. An excavation in 1800 left a large central hollow measuring 1.2 metres deep with a small, recent cairn on the eastern lip.

Staylittle Round Barrows

Group of round barrows
Location: West of Staylittle (SN 878 923)
Access: Can be seen from road and footpath

From Llanidloes take the B4518 to and through Staylittle. Directly past Staylittle turn left on the road signposted Llwynygog. After about quarter of a mile the first two barrows (SN 878 923 and SN 877 922) can be seen across the field on the right. A hundred yards further on, the third barrow (SN 880 920) can be seen on top of a slope to the left. After about another 300 yards the fourth barrow (SN 877 920) is visible from the entrance to Llwyn y gog Farm on the right, looking back toward the house. The fifth barrow (SN 881 915) can be accessed via a rough trail from the entrance to the farm. The sixth barrow (SN 874 908) can be found about three-quarters of a mile beyond the fifth, over two cattle grids, on the right side of the trail.

The barrows of the Staylittle or Penfforddlas group occupy relatively low-lying positions on the sides and in the bottom of a pass running north/south between the Clywedog valley and the Llwyd, one of its tributaries. Several of them were probably intervisible

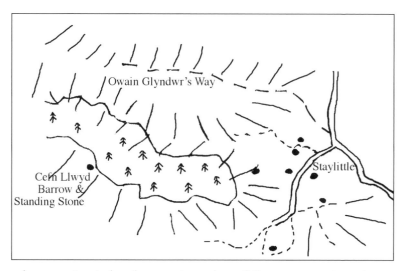

when constructed, subsequent erosion of the monuments and tree planting making this difficult to determine. The barrows are all large and some of them have been disturbed. The first measures 22 by 16 metres and is 1.8 metres tall. The second is 17 metres across and 1.2 metres tall, and a middle Bronze Age urn containing a cremation was found in its centre. Both of these barrows are turf-covered and are located on level ground. The third barrow stands on a north-west facing slope in a false crest position and measures 20 metres north-east to south-west and 16 metres across. This cairn is turf-covered and disturbed by a modern boundary bank in the south-east quadrant. The fourth barrow measures 29.5 metres across and 1.9 metres tall, is set on level ground and is undisturbed. The fifth barrow, measuring 20 metres across and 1.6 metres tall, stands on the crest of a west facing slope from which all the other barrows were probably intervisible. The turf-covered sixth barrow measures 20 metres across and is 1.6 metres high. This barrow is some distance from the others, but would have been intervisible with the fifth barrow if there was no intervening tree growth.

Cefn Llwyd Barrow
and Standing Stone

Barrow and recumbent Standing Stone
Location: West of Staylittle (SN 848 923)
Access: On open hillside, but approach by public paths disrupted by fences and forestry

From Llanidloes take the B4518 to and through Staylittle. Directly past Staylittle turn left on the road signposted Llwynygog. After about half a mile you reach some woodland on the left. Continue past this to the open valley beyond, parking near the farm drive reached soon afterwards on the right hand side (and opposite a track which leads up the hillside to the left).

Walk up the farm track, turning right as soon as you enter the farmyard, and then left shortly after leaving the farmyard, this track leading you diagonally across the hillside. Once through a gate, the track soon bends to double back on itself, but the line of the public footpath continues ahead and shadows the line of the valley on the left. There is one fence to cross with no stile, and then you should stay to the right of the boggy hollow to continue on a footpath through the forestry ahead. However, the forestry work has sorely damaged the path in places, and it is safer to follow the fence around the edge of the forestry to the left. The barrow is set some tens of yards outside the forestry, on the second rise in the ground that you reach, and is fairly obvious to spot from a distance.

The barrow measures 15 metres in diameter and 1.8 metres tall. It is associated with three or four other 'barrows' on the slopes beyond, though these could be natural land formations. Nearby is a white quartz stone which lies recumbent on a boundary line and so may not be in its original position. It measures 1.3 by 0.8 by 0.4 metres.

Breidden Hillfort

Hillfort
Location: 5 miles north-east of Welshpool (SJ 293 143)
Access: By public footpath

From Welshpool take A483 north toward Oswestry, then take the A458 toward Shrewsbury. Turn left almost opposite the phone box at Trewern onto the road signposted to Criggion. Stay on this 'main' minor road, after about 1½ miles passing to the left of a small wooded knoll. Shortly after this, park at the junction of a little lane off to the right that has a sign saying 'Farm and Residential access only'.

Walk on up this lane, which soon swings left as it passes round Upper Farm. When you reach the 'no through road' sign above the farm, turn right onto the track into the Criggion Estate, bearing left at the fork reached in a couple of hundred yards by a house. Follow this track as it swings left and heads towards a narrow valley. Cross the stile by the gate ahead and carry on up this valley. The track eventually passes through a gate onto more open ground, then swings right. Almost below the saddle on your left, a bridleway is sinposted up towards the saddle, then bears left before it is reached. Soon you have a choice of keeping on the bridleway or bearing half right on the footpath that leads more directly to the prominent Rodney's Pillar. The site of the hillfort is on the slopes around the pillar, most particularly to its south-west.

The Breidden hillfort is located defensively, high on a ridge along the Breidden Hills. Around 1000 BC the first defences, palisades, were constructed, making it one of the oldest defended settlements in Wales. This evidence may reflect temporary habitation during a stressful period rather than permanent settlement.

Early artefacts found include several beautiful star-shaped faience beads dated from 2100–1700 BC and early pottery made from local raw materials comprising barrel-shaped pots, open bowls and short-necked situlate jars dated to around 1050 BC. However, the main settlement phase runs from 800 BC through to 600–700 BC, being then abandoned for a short time after it was burned down around 600 BC.

*An excavation in 1971 removed part of the Iron Age rampart,
revealing that from the Bronze Age. Also seen are three of the
front row of paired postholes, backfilled after their original excavation in 1969 and 1970*

Multiple wall-gullies and stakeholes of a roundhouse

The defence system was a slight bank supported by pairs of timber posts set 1 metre apart in two lines. These posts were burned down at some point and defences rebuilt very shortly thereafter. The bank was then augmented and secured with boulders. A line of support posts was then erected in a continuous trench along the bank. These defences enclosed a permanent settlement of approximately 28 hectares. Inside, the Breidden roundhouses, at 5 to 7 metres in diameter, were smaller than most of their British counterparts which usually range from 7 to 11 metres in diameter. Four-post structures, possible storehouses, were also found. Domestic items found included pottery and tools, whilst prestige items included weapons and personal ornamentation suggesting the presence of an elite group or individual in the settlement. At least one paved rectangular area was found behind the rampart, along with associated pits used for refuse and/or votive deposits and postholes from defensive, domestic or pastoral structures. Metal objects including a bronze pin and ring, a socketed hammer, a socketed knife with copper rivets, fragments of a sword, a small unlooped spearhead and a socketed axe complete with its willow shaft, were all found within the fort. This assemblage of bronze objects at the Breidden reflects the shift in deposition practice from hoards to domestic areas (Arnold). In general, as bounded communities increased in number and tribal territories developed, more and more ceremonial practice was confined within the settlements rather than on their peripheries as in the past (Bradley, 1998). Salt containers of the very coarse pottery style from the Malvern region in Wales were also found. Underneath a pond that post dates the fort were found several waterlogged artefacts, including a large cistern, wooden bowl, sword, pestle and mallet head and lengths of plaited wood-rope. It is thought that this area beneath the pond was open ground at the time of habitation. As in other hillforts, there is evidence of small-scale metalworking at the Breidden.

There were several periods when the hillfort was abandoned, and after one of these the inhabitants built a defensive timber and stone rampart on their return. This consisted of a slight bank supported by pairs of timber posts set 1 metre apart in two lines. These posts were burned down at some point and defences rebuilt very shortly thereafter, the bank being augmented and secured with boulders. A line of support posts was then erected in a continuous trench along the bank. Elaborate construction includes an inturned entrance and guard chambers, as is seen at other hillforts of the time. Another period of abandonment may have followed this phase.

Timber roundhouses found inside the hillfort date from 600–400 BC. In the nearby valley, fields and pathways attest to a bustling agricultural production.

The Iron Age

Economic and political changes swept the world at this time. As in Britain, there was plenty of warfare. Leaders were based in centralized areas that were well defended and supplied. The populace was drawn to these areas by promises of protection, resources and cultural affiliation. These centres of population grew larger and denser during this stressful period. People talked with one another. Ideas grew. Institutionalized education was born. Philosophy, sciences, medicine and the arts flourished. The Iron Age probably represents the time of greatest, fastest cultural growth so far in history. It is also a time of rebellion, inspiring the concept of civil rights for the populace, the right to disagree with the government. This must have been quite a radical change in consciousness.

Although the production of iron is more complex than that of bronze, iron became the dominant metal in 700 BC, due to several factors. The first was that Iron is much more widely available than copper and tin, the raw materials for bronze, which could only be mined in a few places. Secondly, there may have been a desire to divest from the political and economic structures controlling the bronze industry which had resulted in complex long distance exchange networks controlled by a few powerful entities. The third reason lies in iron's technological advantage, being much more durable than bronze, although this was not appreciated at first.

The Iron Age therefore began with the adoption of iron as the preferred metal around 700 BC, and lasted until around AD 43. Apart from a period of temperate weather between 300 and 100 BC, the climate gradually became cooler and wetter. Especially harsh conditions in the uplands led to renewed peat formation making agriculture impossible, as it was in the low lying areas because of poor drainage. This left the slopes for cultivation where depletion of soils was avoided by the application of lime and manure, lengthening the lifespan of cultivation fields. This was a dramatic advancement. Cultivars included barley, wheat, oats and rye, whilst flax, beans and herbs for cooking and dyeing cloth were also grown. Saddle and rotary querns for grinding grain were found in large numbers throughout Britain, and cattle, sheep, pig, goats and fowl were kept. In Montgomeryshire, hillforts were constructed on high ground surrounding the Severn Valley, whilst smaller enclosed settlements were built at lower elevations on valley sides and hillslopes.

During the early Iron Age (700-400 BC), society was fragmented with wide disparities between regional industries and deposition practice and an increase in regional economic self-sufficiency—food, ceramic, metal, wood and textile production were all local. This may have been caused by a breakdown in exchange in the late Bronze Age when population numbers declined due to the harsh climate then prevailing. Stress on land and resources as well as attempts to control the supply of raw materials resulted in increased conflict (Arnold), giving rise to a proliferation of hillforts and smaller defended settlements. Hillforts contained domestic structures and storehouses for storing surplus agricultural products. Round houses usually had stone or wattle-and-daub walls with conical thatched roofs and clay or earth floors. A central fireplace and an occasional clay oven could be found inside, smoke from the fire escaping through the thatched roofs. Wooden looms and querns were numerous, attesting to widespread domestic industry. Wooden ploughs or ards pulled by cattle were used in the fields and reaping hooks were used for harvesting wheat. Other structures included workshops, byres and storehouses. Domestic industries took place in the settlements and included metalworking, pottery making, woodworking and the processing of hides for leather.

Celtic culture was strongly influencing Britain by the start of the Iron Age. Roman and Greek classical writers suggest that the Celts were warlike, as evidenced by hillforts and finds of weaponry, booty and prestige goods. Literature and song are replete with stories of heroes and battles, the latter normally consisting of small skirmishes and raids. A warrior's garb consisted of a large wooden

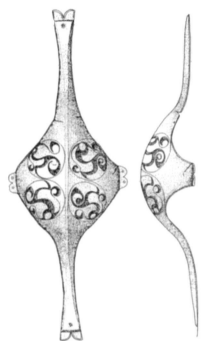

0   16cms

Late Bronze Age or Iron Age metalwork: shield boss found on Anglesey and shield from Merioneth (the latter could even date from the Roman period)

and metal shield and a spear or sword. Fighting was either carried out on foot or from wooden and wicker chariots driven by a charioteer and pulled by a small horse or pony. The warrior would fight standing on the chariot or would jump to the ground for hand-to-hand combat. The chariot could also be used for escape.

It was once thought that the Celts colonized Britain in great numbers during the first millennium BC, introducing Hallstatt and La Tene material cultures and Celtic language. However, it is now thought that the British acquired aspects of Celtic culture by association rather than colonization. There is no doubt that Wales was integrated into the Celtic language zone by at least the first century AD, as Roman documentation indicates Celtic place and tribal names at that time, but there is little evidence that the ancient inhabitants of Britain were related to the central European Celts. Indeed, there is debate as to the validity of the term 'Celtic' in an archaeological and an ethnic sense; the term has been used in conflicting ways by linguists, archaeologists, historians and art historians (Lynch *et al*).

Weaponry: 1 Late Bronze Age sword (Ewart Park type) from Caernarfonshire, which is shorter than the later Iron Age swords.
2, 3, 4 Iron Age swords, 3 with the maker's mark (all three from Anglesey). 5 Dagger from The Breiddin, Montgomeryshire

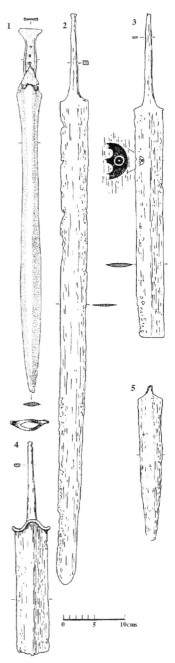

A hierarchy of chiefs and warriors was well established throughout Europe by this time, and a system of clientage and tribute may have been the basis of the relationships between the elite and the farming class, although evidence is ambiguous. It can be deduced, however, that the warrior caste was maintained by a system of favour and reward encouraging bravery and loyalty in which the ability to distribute sought-after goods solidified the power and prestige of the chiefs. Feasting was a popular event of this code as evidenced by finds of numerous drinking cups. A tribe would consist of several kin-groups led by a king or chief, below whom were nobles and skilled men (priests, bards and craftsmen), followed by free men, bondmen and slaves. A system of elective offices was gradually introduced in France, but in Britain the old ways prevailed for quite some time, with minor kings and chiefs remaining in power.

Within this political hierarchy, there was also a hierarchy of religious personnel. Priests were recruited from among the nobles and comprised three sub-classes. The chief priests were Druids. Initiates went through rigorous training and they enjoyed a great deal of power, controlling both secular and ritual life. Some of their power lay in the fact that they enjoyed cross-tribal mobility more than any other member of the group. Caesar considered Druids to be 'a rallying point for national resistance' (Lynch *et al*). They were not warriors, but had tremendous influence over the people in political matters. Diviners or vates comprised the middle religious class, and bards the lowest.

Hillforts were constructed to highlight the chief's power, and so were made as grand as possible. These were major territorial, economic, religious and social centres of population. The size of the hillfort also reflected the agricultural viability of the surrounding landscape. The primary rampart at Breidden was not built until at least 700 BC. Dinorben, occupied since 800 BC, was not defended until 460 BC. Moel-y-Gaer was surrounded by a palisade by 620 BC, followed by a more substantial rampart around 580 BC. These ramparts were vital for sustaining raids, which were probably a primary component of late Bronze Age warfare (Darvill).

Outside the hillforts were many small embanked farmsteads. In the Marches it is believed that the chiefs of the major hillforts presided over an alliance of clans, but that in other parts of Wales the smaller hillforts and embanked farmsteads represent scattered clans presided over by several petty chiefs (Lynch *et al*). Social subdivision is evidenced, although clientage has not been proven with certainty. Two gang-chains discovered at Llyn Cerrig Bach, Anglesey, would have been used either on prisoners of war (Lynch *et al*) or on slaves.

During the middle Iron Age, tribal territories begin to develop. Within these territories, smaller, dispersed communities were united under a centralized power, thus forming a new political/economic structure necessitated by population growth, pressure on resources and the resulting need for protection against rival groups. Ffridd Faldwyn and Cefn Carned, both in Montgomeryshire, had annexes built onto the main forts during this time, indicating accommodation for a larger community during times of stress. Montgomeryshire was probably on the border between the Ordovices tribal territory and that of the Cornovii territory in the Marches.

After 400 BC, hillfort construction and occupation decreased. In a given region, one hillfort probably would remain pre-eminent while the others went out of use. These later hillforts had interior zoning separating domestic structures in one area of the hillfort from storehouses in another. During the late Iron Age, contact with the continent was restricted and at times completely cut off due to the Roman expansion into Gaul. This had a marked effect on southern England which up till then had exported goods and raw materials procured from throughout Britain, including gold, slaves and cattle. Indeed, hillforts in the Marches may have been maintained to provide protection against their southern English neighbours in their quest for gold and slaves. This disruption in trade prompted the tribes in southern England to provide military support to Gaul in their fight for independence against Julius Caesar. Caesar later used this as an excuse to attack the British in 55 and 54 BC (Faulkner).

The many smaller enclosed settlements, usually defended by banks and ditches, were probably farming complexes. Several hundred of these sites are known in the Severn Valley alone, suggesting a large and prosperous population, but the relationship between these smaller farms and hillforts is still ambiguous. Isolated settlements also existed outside both hillforts and these smaller enclosures.

During the Iron Age specialization increased in all crafts. Products were becoming standardized and a system of weights was developed facilitating fair exchange (Arnold). This is evidenced by VCP (very coarse pottery) from the Malverns which was manufactured exclusively for the salt producing industries of Droitwich and Cheshire. The inhabitants of Montgomeryshire regularly imported salt and these containers have been found at Ffryd Faldwyn, the Breidden, Cefn Carnedd, Collfryn, Arddleen, and Llwyn Brin Dinas, all in Montgomeryshire.

Votive depositions were still made and watery sites retained their lure, but it appears that iron never replaced bronze for use in such offerings. However the lack of evidence could be due to the poor survival of iron in water (Arnold). The ditches around sanctuaries also became a favoured location. Llin Cerrig Bach on Anglesey is the site of one of the most spectacular deposits in Britain, reinforcing the idea that Anglesey was a Druidic stronghold. More than 200 items were found during excavation including weaponry (both functional and parade), chariots, horse fittings, smiths' tools, slave chains and animal bones. The artefacts are dated to the years from the 3rd century BC through to 60 AD, indicating continual use. In addition to watery places, Iron Age deposits are often found in sanctuary ditches. Over the period there is also increasing evidence of human and animal sacrifice, which Lynch interprets as showing an increase in religious fervour. Sacrificial victims have been found under ramparts, such as a young male buried alive at Maiden Castle, Dorset (Lynch *et al*).

Diverse burial practices developed during the early Iron Age, although special burial monuments were not constructed. Rituals were performed almost exclusively within settlements. Human bones found in pits are interpreted as fertility rituals rather than evidence of funereal traditions. Animals were often found in similar contexts. During the middle and later Iron Age there was a renewal in formal burial practice outside settlements, and from 100 BC onwards there is evidence for burial of elite members of society as grave goods became more elaborate. Throughout the period, Welsh burials were placed in and around hillforts, often in ditches, and included men, women and children. The position of the corpses varied, however, some flexed or extended (pulled to lie flat), others more 'casually treated' (Lynch *et al*). Some burials were added to earlier religious sites, such as at Devil's Quoit at Stackpole, Pembrokeshire, where one burial was made close to the standing stone and three children near by. Similar activity takes place throughout Wales, including Ystrad Hynod, Trefelgwys, Montgomeryshire. Ystrad Hynod comprised a barrow and standing stone located on a valley floor. Unfortunately, since the excavation all traces of these have been destroyed as the valley has been flooded to create a reservoir. Evidence indicated continued use from Mesolithic times through to the Iron Age (Apsimmon), which could either represent a continuing religious tradition lasting through thousands of years, or a return to the old ways. Later Iron Age burials are unmarked, making them difficult to find. This, rather than their absence, could explain their scarcity in the archaeological record.

Man-made wooden temples began to appear in Britain in the later part of the period, often located near sacred sites such as springs or former monuments. Caves were probably also used. Shrines may have been located in hillforts, but evidence is scarce.

Roman, Irish and Welsh texts, subsequently filtered through a Christian lens, indicate a belief in gods and goddesses. Goddesses represent land and are territorial, whilst gods represent and protect the tribe and are mobile. Legend often has them marrying. Many are manifestations of the forces of nature and agricultural cycle, exhibiting both good and evil characteristics. Several sky gods have been identified including Taranis with his thunderbolts, along with sun gods represented by the wheel, Cernunnos—the horned god of the animals, and a mother goddess with her cornucopia. The chariot wheels found in the deposition at Llin Cerrig Bach may represent the sun god (Lynch). These gods reflect the basic Indo-European pantheon traceable throughout Europe. In addition there were local deities who presided over sacred spots such as springs or wells.

Reconstructed Iron Age dwelling at Castell Henllys,
Pembrokeshire

Animals, especially horses, continue to feature prominently in the pantheon and iconography as tribal totems or as attributes of certain gods (Lynch).

Hillforts are the outstanding remains of Iron Age Montgomeryshire, of which Llanymynech Hill is the largest at 56 hectares. Small scale bronze working for the local community took place in close proximity to this site as copper ore could be obtained from the hillside. Other large hillforts include the Breidden, Ffridd Faldwyn and Cefn Carnedd.

As in the rest of Britain, enclosed smaller sites were discovered with varying layouts, sizes and defensive systems (Arnold). An example of one of these sites can be seen at Colfryn, Llansantffraid-ym-mechair, Montgomeryshire. The site is dated to the middle Iron Age and is enclosed by no fewer than three ditches and banks, with a gated entryway. Three or four roundhouses and several four-post structures, probably granaries, were found inside. One of the round-houses was set apart by its own ditch and bank leading archaeologists to believe that this may have been the principal domestic structure. The arrangement suggests a single extended family, probably of relatively high status. They would have supported themselves on a mixed agricultural economy including animal husbandry and cereal cultivation—cattle, sheep, pig, wheat, barley and oats have left their evidence.

After a period of abandonment around 1000 BC, a defensive timber and stone rampart was constructed at the Breidden. Elaborate construction includes an inturned entrance and guard chambers, similar to other hillforts of the time. Timber round-houses found inside date from 600-400 BC. In the nearby valley, fields and pathways attest to a bustling agricultural production. Several waterlogged artefacts were preserved within a later pond inside the hillfort, including a large cistern, wooden bowl, sword, pestle and mallet head and lengths of plaited wood-rope. It is thought that the area where the pond now lies was open ground at the time of habitation (Arnold). As in other hillforts, there is evidence of small-scale metalworking.

At Ffrydd Faldwyn, timber storehouses lined the roadway near the western entrance of the camp. One wonders if these had any strategic significance. In the early Iron Age a rampart and ditch replaced the Bronze Age double palisade defensive system, a ditch that was recut several times, indicating continued use of the fort. The rampart was eventually burnt down. Part of an early Iron Age vase-headed pin and a decorated stone spindle whorl were discovered at the site (Arnold).

Approximately 300 ditched enclosures have been recorded in the upper Severn Valley. These enclosures usually span from the Iron Age through the Roman Age. The Collfryn, located on a hilltop near Llansantffraid Deuddwr, is a defended farmstead thought to have been constructed in the 3rd to 4th centuries BC. A central area probably contained several timber roundhouses and four and six-post timber storehouses. The elaborate defence system consisted of three widely spaced concentric ditches, suggesting a high-status settlement, possibly that of a chief. This was a productive, industrious camp: there is evidence of cattle, sheep and pig husbandry; cultivars included wheat, barley and oats; and Iron and bronze metalworking were also performed close by. The evidence suggests that the camp was able to sustain itself autonomously. By the first century BC, Collfryn was reduced in size, but occupation appears to have continued until at least the fourth century AD.

Ffrydd Faldwyn Hillfort

Hillfort
Location: On the edge of Montgomery (SO 216 969)
Access: By public footpath

From Montgomery take the back road from the left of the Town Hall to Llandysil and the castle. Follow this up around the town to the castle, parking either as for the castle, or somewhere beyond near the crest of the road.

Walk to the crest in the road, where a footpath leads off to the right across a field to an entrance into the hillfort. This footpath diagonally crosses the site.

Ffrydd Faldwyn hillfort is an impressive example of Iron Age causewayed enclosures that are found all over Britain. Much earlier human activity is postulated for the site, however. One of the enclosure ditches yielded a possible ritual deposition including Peterborough Ware sherds, a polished axe flake and flintwork including an arrowhead and a scraper dating the site to the middle Neolithic when populations expanded into the valley sides of

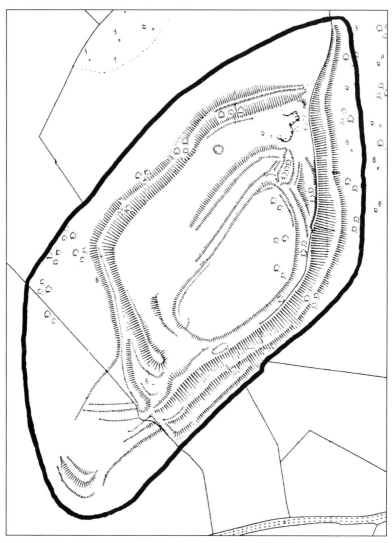

Montgomeryshire. As at Breiddin, Ffrydd Faldwyn was probably first defended by around 1000 BC. These defences may have been allowed to deteriorate for a short period and then reconstructed during the main Iron Age phase of activity, when a rampart and ditch replaced the Bronze Age double palisade defensive system. The ditch was re-cut several times, indicating continued use of the fort. The rampart was eventually burnt down.

During the middle Iron Age, tribal territories began to develop. Within these territories, smaller, dispersed communities were united under a centralized power, thus forming a new political/economic structure necessitated by population growth, pressure on resources and the resulting need for protection against rival groups. Ffrydd Faldwyn and Cefn Carnedd had annexes built onto the main forts during this time, indicating accommodation for a larger community during times of stress. At Ffrydd Faldwyn, timber storehouses lined the roadway through the western entrance of the camp. Part of an early Iron Age vase-headed pin and a decorated stone spindle whorl were discovered at the site (Arnold).

The site today is an irregular oval tapering to the north and south, measuring 950 by 700 feet, 10 acres in area. Within, the area is fairly level, but falls sharply outside the wall to a shallow ditch. A low bank is found on the counterscarp, and a second ditch is found 40 to 60 feet below. The outer enclosure consists of a double rampart and ditch with complex entrance and outworks at the south-west where the ditch deepens to 3 feet, and a second simple undefended entrance at north. These earthworks surround another enclosure in the interior consisting of denuded and very low banks and ditches, but whether this was an earlier, smaller enclosure or formed part of a double defensive structure built at the same time is not known. The outer earthworks are largely wooded and over-grown with gorse and scrub.

And information never remains static. As this book was going to print, several flint tools and animal bones with signs of butchery were being discovered in the Cromer Forest Beds of East Anglia dating to at least 580,000 years ago. At Happisburgh, the first site to be investigated, at least 30 struck flakes, including a beautiful, almost perfect, glossy black handaxe have been found *in situ*, making this the site of the earliest known human activity in Britain, and perhaps in the whole of Northern Europe to use this then advanced handaxe technology.

Bibliography

Aldhouse-Green, Stephen, (ed.), *Paviland Cave and The 'Red Lady', A Definitive Report*, Western Academic and Specialist Press, London, 2000.

Apsimmon, A.M., 'The Excavation of a Bronze Age Barrow and a Menhir at Ystrad-Hynod, Llanidloes (Montgomeryshire)', *Archaeologia Cambrensis* 122, 1965–66.

Arnold, C.J., 'Fridd Faldwyn, Montgomery: The Neolithic Phase', *Archaeologia Cambrensis* 136, 1987.

The Archaeology of Montgomeryshire, The Powysland Club, Welshpool, 1990.

Bradley, Richard, *An Archaeology of Natural Places*, Routledge, London, 2000.

Rock Art and The Prehistory of Atlantic Europe, Routledge, London, 1997.

The Significance of Monuments, Routledge, London, 1998.

The Moon & The Bridge, Society of Antiquaries, Edinburgh, 2005

Burnham, Helen, *A Guide to Ancient and Historic Wales: Clwyd and Powys*, CADW, HMSO, London, 1995.

Chamberlain, A.T, 'Early Neolithic dates on human bone from Fox Hole Cave, Derbyshire', Capra 3, 2001 available at http://www.shef.ac.uk/~capra/3/foxholedates.html.

Clarke, David, *Skara Brae*, Historic Scotland, Edinburgh, 1996.

Clottes, Jean and Lewis-Williams, David, *The Shamans of Prehistory*, Harry N. Abrams Pub. NYC, 1996.

Darvill, Timothy, *Prehistoric Britain*, Routledge, London, 1987.

Dorling, Peter: 'Llyn y Tarw Stone Circle, Aberhafesp, Montgomeryshire', *Archaeologia Cambrensis* 131, 1982.

Drury, Nevill, *Shamanism*, Element Books Ltd., Massachusetts, 1996.

Dyer, James, *Discovering Archaeology in England and Wales*, Shire Publications, Risborough, 2002.

Faulkner, Neil, 'Sedgeford, Treasure of the Iceni', *Current Archaeology* 192, June 2004.

Ferriby Boats Website, http://www.ferribyboats.co.uk/dating

Gamble, Clive, *The Palaeolithic Societies of Europe*, Cambridge University Press, 1999.

Gibson, Alex, 'The Stone Row of Cerrig yr Helfa, Mynydd Dyfnant, Powys', *CPAT* 24, 1992.

'Earlier Prehistoric Funerary and Ritual Sites in the Upper Severn Valley', *The Montgomeryshire Collections*, Journal of the Powysland Club 90, 2002.

'Excavations at Coed y Dinas, Welshpool, Powys' February, 1992, CPAT 65, 1993.

'Survey and Excavation at a Newly Discovered Long Barrow at Lower Lugwy, Berriew, Powys', *Studia Celtica* 34, University of Wales Press, Cardiff, 2000.

'The Excavation of a Ring Ditch at Elmtree Farm', *Archaeology in Wales* 32, Council for British Archaeology, Wales, 1992.

'The Excavation of a Structured Cairn at Carneddau, Near Carno, Powys', *CPAT* 5, 1989.

'The Excavation of the Timber Circle and Horseshoe-Shaped Enclosure at Sarn-y-bryn-caled, Near Welshpool, Powys: An Interim Report', *The Montgomeryshire Collections*, Journal of the Powysland Club 80, Gomer Press, Llandysul, 1992.

Gifford, Edwin and Gifford, Joyce: 'The Ferriby Ship Experiment', *Current Archaeology* 191, April 2004.

Goodman, Morris and Moffatt, Anne, eds., *Probing Human Origins*, American Academy of Arts and Sciences, Cambridge, MA, 2002.

Jacobi, R., Parfitt, S., and Stringer, C., 'The Ancient Human Occupation of Britain', *Current Archaeology* 190, February 2004.

Johnson, F., 'The Nest, Four Crosses, Powys', *CPAT* 548, June 2003.

Larick, Roy and Ciochon, Russell L., 'The African Emergence and Early Asian Dispersals of the Genus Homo', *American Scientist*, Nov-Dec 1996.

Lynch, Frances, *Megalithic Tombs and Long Barrows*, Shire Archaeology, Buckinghamshire, 2004.

& Aldhouse-Green, Stephen; Davies, Jeffrey, *Prehistoric Wales*, Sutton Publishing Ltd., Gloucestershire, 2000.

Marshack, Alexander, 'The Berekhat Ram Figurine: A Late Acheulian Carving From The Middle East', *Antiquity* 71, June 1997.

The Roots of Civilization, 2nd Edition, Moyer Bell Ltd., Mt. Kisko, NY, 1991.

McNabb, John, *An Archaeological Resource Assessment and Research Agenda for the Palaeolithic in the East Midlands (part of Western Doggerland)*, University of Leicester, 2004.

Mills, Susan: 'Alloa: A Bronze Age Woman and an Iron Age Warrior', *Current Archaeology* 191, April 2004.

Mithen, Steven, *The Prehistory of the Mind*.

Myers, A.M., *An Archaeological Resource Assessment and Research Agenda For the Mesolithic in the East Midlands*, Chapter 3, University of Leicester at http://www.le.ac.uk/archaeology /pdf_files/emidmeso.pdf

Pearce, P., Reed, S., 'Late Bronze Age Pottery Making at Sherborne', *Current Archaeology* 188, October 2003.

Pettitt, P.B., 'Discovery, Nature and Preliminary Thoughts About Britain's First Cave Art', University of Sheffield, *Capra* 5 available at http://www.shef.ac.uk/~capra/5/pettitt.html.

Potts, Richard: 'Complexity and Adaptability in Human Evolution'.

Rudgeley, Richard, *Lost Civilizations of the Stone Age*, Touchstone Books, NYC, 1999.

Shreeve, James, *The Neanderthal Enigma*, Avon Books, NYC, 1995.

Silvester, R.J. and Davies, G., 'A Lithic Scatter on Mynydd Carreg-y-Big, Llanerfyl', T*he Montgomeryshire Collections*, Journal of the Powysland Club 80, Gomer Press, Llandysul, 1992.

Smithsonian Institution Website: http://www.mnh.si.edu/anthro/ humanorigins/ha/a_tree.html

St. Edmundsbury County Website: http://www.stedmundsbury.gov.uk/ sebc/visit/beginning-of-man.cfm

The Welsh Lower Palaeolithic Survey, Trust for Wessex Archaeology, Wiltshire, 1996.

Thomas, Julian, *Understanding the Neolithic*, Routledge, London, 2001.

Wood, Jacqui: 'Bunsen Burners or Cheese Moulds?', *Current Archaeology* 191, April 2003.

Also from Logaston Press

The Folklore of Shropshire
by Roy Palmer
ISBN 1 904396 16 X

Shropshire's folklore is presented in a series of themed chapters that encompass landscape, buildings, beliefs, work, seasons, people, music and drama. In the eleven chapters the county's rich store of folklore unfolds in a way that allows you to dip into what most intrigues, or to read from start to finish. Here are stories of mark stones, stone circles, giants, tunnels, dragons, rivers, meres, pools, hills, church sites changed by the devil, vengeful spirits, bull and bear baiting, cockfighting, fairs, herbal remedies and those which involve peculiar activities, minstrels, histriones, waits, charmers and 'cunning folk', ghosts, witches, bountiful cows, of characters such as the early saints, Caratacus, Edric the Wild, Humphrey Kynaston, Jack Mytton and even recent folklore surrounding Hilda Murrell, of tales of the Civil War and of Hopton Quarter, of celebrations and customs surrounding times such as Easter, Christmas, All Souls' Eve, Ascension Day and Palm Sunday along with the likes of 'burning the mawkin', 'tin panning' and wife selling, of rhymes that link villages, ballads that tell of events in the county's past, of folk plays and mummers—to mention just some of what is included.

Roy Palmer is nationally known for his researches into folklore and in 2004 he was awarded the English Folk Dance and Song Society's highest honour, its gold badge.

Over 250 photographs, drawings and samples of music.

Price £12.95

Also from Logaston Press

Prehistoric Sites of Breconshire
by George Children and George Nash
ISBN 1 873827 57 1

This is the fourth book in this Monuments in the Landscape series written by George Children and George Nash, the research for this and the previous volumes (on Herefordshire, on Monmouthshire and on the Neolithic Sites of Cardiganshire, Carmarthenshire and Pembrokeshire) serving to develop their view that many monuments left by our prehistoric ancestors show distinct regional variations.

Prehistoric Breconshire played host to hunter/gatherers spreading up the river valleys, first establishing temporary encampments before their descendants decided to settle and start to farm the lowland areas.

Much of the early settlement took place in the shadows of the Black Mountains which appear to have formed a unifying feature, providing a sense of a shared 'territory' between the various early tribes or families. With the advent of the use of Bronze, coupled with an improvement in the climate, man spread out across what became Breconshire and moved up the hillsides to live, farm — and be buried. In the Iron Age the highest ground was vacated as the climate deteriorated, and habitation and activity was concentrated along the river valleys, notably of the Usk and its tributaries. As the story unfolds so the authors establish a feeling for early man's lifestyle, beliefs and customs.

This book is divided into three sections — The Stone Ages, The Bronze Age and the Iron Age. Each section is followed by individual guides to the more important and often more accessible sites, including Neolithic burial monuments, Bronze Age religious sites and Iron Age hillforts.

With some 100 photographs, maps, plans and drawings.

Price £7.95

Also from Logaston Press

The Architecture of Death—
The Chambered Tombs of Wales
by George Nash
ISBN 1 904396 33 X

This book details the 100 chambered tombs within Wales that have significant remains.

An opening chapter details the background to the Neolithic, or new stone age, when these tombs were built. It covers the climate and vegetation of the period, the changing cultural influences, the trade contacts by sea with Ireland and Brittany and thence further afield, as well as overland through what became western England. The culture and beliefs of the people are considered, the scant evidence for their settlements contrasting with the often dramatic remains of the monuments for their dead. The five different styles of chambered tombs are described—Portal Dolmens, the Cotswold-Severn Tradition, Passage Graves, Gallery Graves and Earth-Fast monuments—with thoughts as to why the varied styles developed in the way and locations that they did. There is still much to consider: for example the bones found in some tombs often prove to be the assorted remains of a number of individuals. Does this mean that people were initially buried elsewhere and subsequently moved to a main, central tomb, with bones being lost in the process? Was it just the social elite who were buried in these tombs, and if so what happened to the rest of society?

The bulk of the book is a gazetteer to the 100 sites, with copious plans and photographs, along with a description and summary of what is known from the various archaeological excavations and research that has taken place over the years.

George Nash is a part-time lecturer at the Department of Archaeology and Anthropology, University of Bristol. He is also a Principal Archaeologist at Gifford (Chester). George has researched the Neolithic and Mesolithic over most of Europe.

Over 220 photographs, plans and drawings
Price £17.50